Cas Clarke wrote her first book, *Grub on a Grant*, after taking a degree in Urban Studies at Sussex University. She now lives in a rural retreat in Surrey with her husband Andy, baby son James and their mad cat and dog, Matti and Barney.

Also by Cas Clarke

Grub on a Grant
Feast Your Friends
Peckish but Poor
Mean Beans
Sainsbury's Quick and Easy Cooking for Students

Posh Nosh

Cooking for
Special Occasions

Cas Clarke

HEADLINE

For my biggest fan – my mother

First published in 1995
by HEADLINE BOOK PUBLISHING

10 9 8 7 6 5 4 3 2 1

ISBN 0 7472 4568 1

Typeset by
Letterpart Limited, Reigate, Surrey

Printed and bound in Great Britain by
Cox & Wyman Ltd, Reading, Berkshire

HEADLINE BOOK PUBLISHING
A division of Hodder Headline PLC
338 Euston Road
London NW1 3BH

Contents

Raw eggs

The Department of Health advises that babies, elderly people, those pregnant or ill should not eat dishes – for example hollandaise sauce or meringues – containing raw eggs but that any eggs should be thoroughly cooked until both the yolk and white are solid. For other people there is very little risk from eating eggs cooked by any method; raw eggs, however, are not advised.

Introduction

How do you cope when it is your turn to have the family for Christmas dinner? When you have to cook Sunday lunch for the in-laws for the first time? What are you going to do when you realize your parents' silver wedding anniversary is looming or your vegetarian daughter is getting married and you have no ideas for the wedding breakfast?

These are problems that come to most of us at some time or other – however, they can be very pleasurable to solve, and in doing so we reap our reward with the pleasure of the actual event and the knowledge that we are providing for those we love. Of course, all some people have to do is call in the caterer – but this is not always an option, and if you can cope you will find that you can produce a spread that is far superior to the one a caterer could provide for the same budget. I actually catered for my own wedding (with help on the day), knowing that it was the only way that we could have the luxury dishes that I wanted to provide. For an equivalent budget a caterer could have provided only a very basic spread.

Of course, families do not come together only for the big occasions. Other popular family get-togethers are Sunday lunch and birthday celebrations – occasions which are easy to make special with just a little foresight.

Although we can never rely on the British weather, barbecues are now a very popular part of our lives. I'm sure that their growth in popularity has come about because of their simplicity – most of the work is done beforehand, and unless the chicken is raw inside or the sausages are completely frazzled, we can't help getting it right!

The idea behind this book, as in all my books, is

simplicity. Being basically of a very lazy nature, I will always take the easy way of doing something. For this book I have attempted some dishes which are a bit special and require a little more time and effort than in the past – but nothing my guinea-pig (Andy!) couldn't cope with. So as always, I feel certain that if he can do it – so can you!

Organization

For these occasions to be happy ones, it is essential that you get yourself organized beforehand. Only if you are feeling confident that you have forgotten nothing and left nothing to chance will you be able to relax and actually enjoy the occasion yourself. Therefore, planning is necessary to ensure that you reach this happy state.

The rules are simple:

1 Decide on the venue, guests and date of the event.
2 Decide what can you afford.
3 Think about how much help you will have – before, on the day and afterwards (someone has to clear up).

Once these basics have been sorted out you need to plan the whole event meticulously, from where people will park, to where they will leave their coats, to making sure you have enough loo paper, to where the family pets will be kept. For outdoor events, you must decide on alternative plans if the weather proves problematic. At this stage try to be pessimistic – some problems can safely be ignored, but you may discover some real obstacles. For example, will 60 people actually fit into your house? If people are eating a fork buffet standing up, where will they put their glasses? For a toddlers' tea – what will parents do while waiting for their offspring? The planning should take place well before the event so that you have plenty of time to iron out all the things that can go wrong.

Two words of warning here! First, in my experience, however much effort you put into the planning, the chances are that something unexpected will still happen on the day. At a recent party we gave, for instance, even though we had specially rung the hire company to get the dimensions of the trestle tables we had ordered, when they actually arrived they were slightly larger than we had been told – and wouldn't therefore fit into the space where we were expecting to put them. We had to rearrange our plans quickly, and then found that we didn't have enough tablecloths! Luckily the hire company were very good and quickly sent someone over with another cloth.

Second, a word on budgeting for your event. I have never, ever found an event to work out cheaper than I had planned, so be warned and be realistic as to what you can afford. Basically, the more people you invite the higher the cost will be. So if you are determined to have a very posh affair, you will have to keep the numbers down if your budget is limited.

This book has been specifically aimed at family affairs. During our lives there are many events that occur and which need marking in a special way. They are part of our transition through the different stages of life. Throughout the world you will find that people celebrate these occasions with food and drink. They are important events. It is unfortunate that in this country many of these occasions have become very expensive to celebrate. Events that were once simply marked have become very commercialized. Consider the cost nowadays of the average wedding and Christmas and you will see what I mean.

I think this is a terrible shame, and I feel that people would get a lot more pleasure from these events if they simplified them – and in the process saved themselves money. What I have given in this book are some of our very best family recipes, and I hope also to give you some ideas on how to make these occasions special ones for you and your family – at a reasonable cost. The menus for each chapter give suggestions for suitable recipes for each occasion; extra ideas are given at the end of the menu pages.

Quantities

If you are planning a family meal for numbers ranging from 4–8 you should have no problem estimating the quantities involved. As soon as you start to look at numbers larger than this, however, the quantities change. They will alter according to the type of party you are planning, and to the age and sex of the guests involved.

As a general rule, the higher the number of guests involved, the less per head you need to allow. This holds particularly true of vegetable and salad dishes. Another point that needs to be taken into account, however, is that if you are offering a choice of main courses, you must allow for the fact that most people will have a little of both choices – thus you will need to allow a little more per head. I always allow a little extra for any particularly greedy guests, and I have never had any problems finding a home for any leftovers!

Planning

Let me give you a run-down on how you might organize an event. As an example, I will use a recent party we had as part of my mother's 60th birthday celebrations.

4

1 First, my mother gave me a list of guests, and invitations were ordered and sent out.
2 Next, I decided on a menu, taking into account that it was to be a midweek celebration and that, being very pregnant, there was a limit to what I could personally undertake. Therefore I decided that some of the menu would have to be bought in.
3 We decided how we would decorate the house and lay up the buffet table, and measured up the rooms. Then we bought decorations, and ordered flowers and everything necessary for the buffet – including trestle tables, tablecloths, serving platters, cutlery, crockery, glasses, punch bowls, etc.
4 After having got the replies back to the invitations it was estimated that we would have between 36–40 guests in the evening. Since we were offering a choice of 3 courses (salmon, coronation chicken and cold meats), this meant allowing 40 buffet-sized portions of each dish. Therefore we decided to make up 40 portions of the coronation chicken and ordered the salmon and cold meats.
5 The quantities for salads and desserts were worked out and we also ordered platters of nibbles from a local supermarket deli so that we wouldn't have to prepare these ourselves.
6 We allowed ⅔ of a bottle of wine per person plus a glass of champagne, with additional beers and lagers for those who prefer these to wine. (If you are planning a party of more than 50 people you can allow ½ a bottle per person.) I also planned two non-alcoholic punches for non-drinkers. Thus we ordered 2½ cases of wine and ½ a case of champagne to be on the safe side.
7 I baked the cake and started 'feeding' it.
8 In the week preceding the party, my mother cleared away as much as possible from the hall and

kitchen, so that we would have room for the glasses, etc. when they arrived, and to make room for people's coats. I made shopping lists, checking and re-checking the ingredients against my chosen menu to ensure that nothing had been forgotten.

9 The party was to be on Wednesday. On Sunday when I arrived at my mother's I marzipanned the cake, so that it would be ready to ice the following day.

10 On Monday, we did the shopping and spent the afternoon making the coronation chicken. I also iced the cake.

11 On Tuesday, Andy put up the decorations. My mother and I made up the salads and I started on the desserts. We checked the crockery, etc. when it arrived. I finished decorating the cake with ribbons, lace and 60 candles! When my brother and his wife arrived, they helped Andy finish off the decorations. (We had a Chinese takeaway that night!)

12 On Wednesday everyone helped to lay up and decorate the buffet table. I finished off the desserts. My brother went off to collect the salmon and ice that we had ordered. White wine was put to chill and some red wine was opened.

13 Thirty minutes before the party was due to start, we were all dressed and ready. Ice was added to the punches. We all had a drink to get in the mood!

14 Next day the decorations had to be taken down and the hire company came to collect all the hired crockery, etc. – which we had arranged to return unwashed.

It was a really wonderful party which everyone enjoyed, especially my mother – which after all was the point of the event!

1 Easter

Easter is a welcome occasion and one when many families get together. Although for many people it has lost its religious significance, the four-day break that most people have makes it easier to get to our families. It is a very popular event for children – who of course associate it with school holidays and Easter eggs. It is also the time of the year when seasonal attractions open, so we always like to try and get out at some point in the festivities – though of course the weather doesn't always allow this!

I have given recipes here for a perfect Easter weekend – but as life is rarely perfect, it is best to be prepared and have some alternative plans.

Suggested menus
(Recipes are given in the order shown below)

Good Friday
Friday fish with chunky herb and tomato sauce
Gratin dauphinois
Carrots with lemon and ginger

Fruit and egg custard tart

Drinks
White or rosé wine

Easter picnic
Finger food
Sandwiches
Mini pastries
Onion eggs
Thermos of soup

Carrot and banana cake
Fresh fruit

Drinks
Thermos of tea/coffee
Soft drinks

Posh Easter picnic
Thermos of soup
Sausage and egg plait
Hot 'n' spicy chicken
Selection of salads
Sticky gingerbread
Fruit salad

Drinks
Wine
Canned beers
Soft drinks
Thermos of real coffee

Easter Sunday
Stuffed lamb or turkey Clementine
Roasted new potatoes
Peas à la française
Creamed leeks

Raspberry soufflé

Drinks
Champagne or sparkling wine

Easter Monday
Curried lamb or turkey à la King
Rice

Fruit salad

Drinks
Beer or lager

Other suggested recipes
Shepherd's pie
Turkey Creole
Gado gado
Peanut sauce

Friday fish with chunky herb and tomato sauce
Serves 4–6

This is a very useful fish dish. It is a very apt dish for Easter but in various forms I use this particular recipe on many occasions during the year. You can use various types of fish fillets but our particular favourites are cod or plaice.

4–6 × 8 oz (4–6 × 200 g) fish fillets

Chunky herb and tomato sauce
2 onions, chopped
4 cloves garlic, crushed
4 tablespoons (60 ml) olive oil
2 × 16 oz (2 × 400 g) cans chopped tomatoes
1 tablespoon (15 ml) tomato purée
4 tablespoons (60 ml) chopped fresh parsley
2 tablespoons (30 ml) chopped fresh basil
grated rind and juice of 1 lime
salt and pepper

First make the sauce. Fry the onion and garlic in the oil until soft and starting to colour (about 10 minutes). Now add the rest of the sauce ingredients and simmer for 10 minutes. Meanwhile, pre-heat the oven to 190°C/375°F/Gas 5. Pour the sauce into a large oiled baking dish (a lasagne dish works well) and place the fish fillets on top. Season with salt and pepper. Cover with foil and bake in the pre-heated oven for 15–20 minutes, until the fish is cooked.

Gratin dauphinois
Serves 4–6

2 lb (800 g) potatoes, sliced thinly
knob of butter
salt and pepper
2 cloves garlic, crushed
5 fl oz (125 ml) milk
5 fl oz (125 ml) double cream
2 oz (50 g) Gruyère cheese, grated

Pre-heat the oven to 200°C/400°F/Gas 6. Steam, boil or microwave the potatoes for a few minutes until tender, but not cooked through. (This is known as 'par-boiling'.) Layer into a shallow casserole dish, dotting with butter and seasoning each layer. Mix the garlic with the milk and cream and pour over the potato. Top with cheese. Bake in the pre-heated oven for 45 minutes or until the top is brown.

Carrots with lemon and ginger
Serves 4–6

1–1½ lb (400–600 g) carrots, sliced
grated rind of 1 lemon and 1 tablespoon (15 ml)
    juice
large knob of butter
1 teaspoon (5 ml) ginger purée
chopped fresh parsley

Place all the ingredients except the parsley in a saucepan and just cover with water. Bring to the boil and then cook for 10–15 minutes until the carrots are tender and the water has evaporated. Occasionally give the pan a good shake to prevent the carrots sticking. Watch closely at the end to prevent the carrots burning. Serve sprinkled with the parsley.

Fruit and egg custard tart
Serves 6–8

12 oz (300 g) shortcrust pastry (see page 38)
1 lb (400 g) prepared fruit
2 tablespoons (30 ml) sugar

Custard topping
1 egg and 2 egg yolks
1 oz (25 g) sugar
1 oz (25 g) butter, melted
1 oz (25 g) flour
10 fl oz (250 ml) single cream

Pre-heat the oven to 190°C/375°F/Gas 5. Line an 8 inch (20 cm) flan case with pastry and bake 'blind' for 15–20 minutes. Whisk the eggs, sugar and butter together, add the flour and then the cream. Put the fruit and sugar in the pastry shell and pour in the custard. Cook for a further 20–30 minutes until the custard has set.

Mini pastries
Makes 16–24

These pastries are very quick and easy to make if you have a food processor. However, another alternative is to use filo pastry. Check out the recipe for cheese borek (page 40) to find out how to use it. When using filo, especially with potato fillings, I tend to deep-fry them instead of baking them. They need only a couple of minutes and are good both hot and cold.

2 oz (50 g) cream cheese
4 oz (100 g) butter
6 oz (150 g) plain flour
egg to glaze

Mix the first three ingredients in a food processor and chill. Pre-heat the oven to 200°C/400°F/Gas 6. Roll out the pastry and cut into circles. Fill with 1 teaspoon (5 ml) of your chosen filling, seal and glaze. Cook in the pre-heated oven for 10–15 minutes until brown.

HAM AND MUSHROOM
   thick white sauce (enriched with cream) (see page 14)
   4oz (100g) ham, chopped
   mushrooms cooked in butter
   touch of English mustard
   salt and pepper

Mix the ingredients together.

CHEAT'S CORONATION CHICKEN
   1 boned chicken breast, cooked and skin removed
   1 shallot, finely chopped
   1 clove garlic, crushed
   1 tablespoon (15 ml) oil
   1–2 teaspoons (5–10 ml) curry paste
   pinch of ginger
   1 teaspoon (5 ml) tomato purée
   1–2 teaspoons (5–10 ml) mango chutney
   3 tablespoons (45 ml) mayonnaise
   1 tablespoon (15 ml) single cream

Finely shred the chicken breast. Fry the shallot and garlic
in oil for 3 minutes until soft. Add the spices and tomato
purée and cook for 1 minute. Cool and stir in the other
ingredients.

PEA, POTATO AND MINT
   4 oz (100 g) mashed potato
   2 oz (50 g) cooked peas
   1 oz (25 g) cream cheese
   2 tablespoons (30 ml) chopped fresh mint
   salt and pepper

Mix the ingredients together.

CHEESE, POTATO AND CORIANDER
   4 oz (100 g) mashed potato
   2 oz (50 g) grated cheese
   1 oz (25 g) cream cheese
   1 tablespoon (15 ml) chopped fresh coriander
   salt and pepper

Mix the ingredients together.

White sauce
Makes 10 fl oz (250 ml)

> 1 oz (25 g) butter or margarine
> 1 oz (25 g) flour, sifted
> 10 fl oz (250 ml) milk

Melt the butter or margarine in a small saucepan and then take the pan away from the heat. Add the flour, stir well and then return to a gentle heat, stirring continuously. Add a little of the milk, and keep stirring to ensure lumps do not appear. The mixture will be very thick – keep thinning it gradually with the milk. When all the milk has been incorporated, keep stirring and continue cooking for a minute or two to ensure that the flour is cooked through.

CHEESE SAUCE
Add 2 oz (50 g) grated cheese and a touch of mustard to the sauce.

Onion eggs

This was always part of our Easter preparations when I was a child. We used to love making these and seeing what different effects we could get with the leaves. They have become very popular again, and so have coloured eggs – these are cooked in water with either beetroot or spinach, which colours the whole egg.

> 6 eggs
> onion peel
> string

Carefully bind some onion leaves around the eggs. Bring to the boil and cook for 10 minutes. When the peel is removed you will have hard-boiled eggs with a marbled effect.

Cream of onion soup
Makes 6–8 cups

1½ lb (600 g) onions, finely chopped
2 oz (50 g) butter
1½ pints (750 ml) vegetable or chicken stock
pinch of herbs – tarragon is good
1 tablespoon (15 ml) cornflour
5 fl oz (125 ml) milk
4 tablespoons (60 ml) single cream
salt and pepper

Fry the onions in the butter until soft, about 7–8 minutes. Do not drain them. Add the stock and herbs and bring to the boil. Cover and simmer for 35–40 minutes. Blend or purée the soup and return to the heat. Mix the cornflour with some of the milk and add to the soup with the rest of the milk. Bring to the boil and stir until the soup thickens. Remove from the heat, stir in the cream and season to taste. Store in a Thermos.

Carrot, ginger and lemon soup
Serves 6–8

1 onion, chopped
1 clove garlic, crushed
1 teaspoon (5 ml) ginger purée
1 large knob of butter
1 lb (400 g) carrots, chopped
grated rind and juice of 1 lemon
1 pint (500 ml) vegetable stock
5 fl oz (125 ml) single cream
sprinkling of fresh thyme (optional)
salt and pepper

Fry the onion, garlic and ginger in the butter until just starting to soften. Add the carrots and cover tightly. Turn the heat down and cook for 10 minutes until the carrots soften. Add the lemon and stock and bring to the boil. Cover and simmer for 25 minutes. Purée or blend until smooth, then add the cream and gently heat through, but do not boil. Season to taste and pour into a Thermos.

Carrot and banana cake

The humble carrot cake has been a popular favourite in our house for a long time. However, there always comes a time to move on and I have to admit that since I developed this recipe it has become even more popular than plain carrot cake.

5 oz (125 g) self-raising flour
4 oz (100 g) soft dark brown sugar
4 oz (100 g) soft margarine
3 oz (75 g) ground rice
2 eggs, beaten
4 tablespoons (60 ml) milk
pinch of nutmeg
pinch of cinnamon
1 banana, mashed
10 oz (250 g) carrots, peeled and grated

Pre-heat the oven to 180°C/350°F/Gas 4. Beat the flour, sugar, margarine, ground rice, eggs and milk together. Stir in the rest of the ingredients. Line a 2 lb (800 g) loaf tin with baking parchment and spoon the cake mixture in. Level the top of the mixture. Bake in the pre-heated oven for 55–60 minutes. Leave to cool in the tin for 5 minutes, then remove to a wire rack and cool.

Sausage and egg plait
Serves 4–6

This is a dish that I first made in Domestic Science at school! I have made some changes to the original recipe but the idea behind it is still the same. It is a robust dish, which makes it ideal for picnics. It is also a very good way of using up some of the hard-boiled eggs that the children may have had fun colouring!

   1 lb (400 g) puff pastry
   8 oz (800 g) sausagemeat
   1 tablespoon (15 ml) chopped fresh parsley
   1 tablespoon (15 ml) chopped fresh chives
   1 egg, beaten
   2 tablespoons (30 ml) milk
   4 hard-boiled eggs, shelled
   egg to glaze
   salt and pepper

Pre-heat the oven to 220°C/425°F/Gas 7. Roll out the pastry to an 11 × 9 inch (28 × 23 cm) rectangle. Blend together the sausagemeat, herbs, beaten egg and milk. Season well. Using half this mixture, spread a covering of sausagemeat down the middle third of the pastry. Now lay the hard-boiled eggs down the middle of the pastry. Using the rest of the mixture, encase the eggs completely. Then cut each of the 2 outer sections of pastry into diagonal strips. Cross these strips over the middle section so as to create a plaited effect which encases the eggs and sausagemeat. Pinch the ends down. Glaze with egg and carefully transfer to a greased baking tray. Bake in the pre-heated oven for 20–30 minutes until the pastry is brown. Serve hot or cold in slices.

MUSHROOM AND EGG PLAIT

For a vegetarian alternative to this dish, substitute mushroom pâté for the sausagemeat. For a buffet dish (such as for a vegetarian wedding) I would also substitute quail's eggs for the hard-boiled eggs.

Hot 'n' spicy chicken
Makes 12 drumsticks

> 12 chicken drumsticks, skinned
> 6 fl oz (150 ml) groundnut oil
> 4 cloves garlic, crushed
> 1 onion, finely chopped
> 4 tablespoons (60 ml) natural yoghurt
> 2 tablespoons (30 ml) tomato purée
> pinch of turmeric
> dash of chilli sauce

Put the drumsticks into a container, making deep gashes in each one. Blend the rest of the ingredients together, adding chilli sauce to your taste. Pour the marinade over the chicken and leave for at least 4 hours. Grill for 20 minutes until charred on each side, basting frequently with the marinade.

Sticky gingerbread
Makes 8–10 slices

1 tablespoon (15 ml) golden syrup
6 tablespoons (90 ml) black treacle
3 tablespoons (45 ml) muscovado sugar
4 oz (100 g) soft margarine or butter
8 oz (200 g) plain brown flour
2 teaspoons (10 ml) baking powder
1 teaspoon (5 ml) ground ginger
pinch of mixed spice
2 eggs, beaten
½ teaspoon (3 ml) bicarbonate of soda
5 fl oz (125 ml) milk

Pre-heat the oven to 170°C/325°F/Gas 3. Melt the syrup, treacle, sugar and fat together. Mix in all the dry ingredients except the bicarbonate of soda. Beat in the eggs. Dissolve the bicarbonate of soda in the milk and add to the mixture. Stir well. Put in a greased, lined 2 lb (800 g) loaf tin. Bake in the pre-heated oven for 90 minutes. Cool, wrap in foil, and keep for 5–7 days – it goes very sticky.

Fruit salad
Serves 6–8

3 oz (75 g) caster sugar
8 fl oz (200 ml) water
1 large pineapple, cut into chunks
4 bananas, sliced
4 Sharon fruit, sliced
1 small melon, balled
maraschino cherries, drained
1 liqueur glass of your favourite liqueur

Dissolve the sugar in the water and boil for a few minutes until you have a syrup. Add the fruit and liqueur and chill before serving.

Stuffed lamb
Serves 6–8

Do not ask your butcher to bone the lamb when he is extremely busy and there is a long queue behind you – either forewarn him, or make sure you go at a quieter time. Of course, you could attempt to bone the lamb yourself. It is something I have done in the past, but unlike boning a chicken, I think this is quite difficult. I thoroughly advise you to ask the butcher to do it.

4 lb (1.6 kg) leg of lamb, boned
knob of butter
few slices of onion

Stuffing
4 oz (100 g) fresh breadcrumbs
4 oz (100 g) no-soak dried apricots, chopped
1 small onion, finely chopped
1 tablespoon (15 ml) chopped fresh parsley
1 egg, beaten
salt and pepper

Pre-heat the oven to 180°C/350°F/Gas 4. Mix together the stuffing ingredients and use to stuff the lamb. Sew up with fine string. Melt the fat and place the joint in a roasting tin with the fat and the onion slices. Baste. Bake in the pre-heated oven for 2 hours, basting occasionally.

Turkey Clementine
Serves 6–8

12 lb (4.8 kg) oven-ready turkey
butter
salt and pepper

Stuffing
8 oz (200 g) onion, chopped
2 oz (50 g) butter
2 tablespoons (30 ml) chopped fresh parsley
grated rind of 1 lemon and 2 tablespoons (30 ml)
    juice
grated rind of 1 orange and 2 tablespoons (30 ml)
    juice
4 oz (100 g) fresh white breadcrumbs
salt and pepper

Pre-heat the oven to 220°C/425°F/Gas 7. Cook the onion in the butter until just soft (about 6 minutes). Mix with the other stuffing ingredients and use to stuff the neck end of the turkey. Lay some foil in your roasting tin and place the turkey on this. Spread the turkey liberally with butter and sprinkle with the rest of the juice from the lemon and the orange. Season. Wrap loosely with the foil. Put in the pre-heated oven for 30 minutes. Turn the oven temperature down to 170°C/325°F/Gas 3 and cook for 3 hours. Finally, remove the foil and turn the heat back up to 200°C/400°F/Gas 6 for 30 minutes to brown the skin. Leave to rest on a warm plate for 30–40 minutes before carving.

Roasted new potatoes
Serves 6–8

2 lb (800 g) new potatoes, halved
olive oil
2 sprigs fresh rosemary, chopped
3 cloves garlic, crushed
juice of ½ a lemon
salt and pepper

Place the potatoes in a bowl with enough oil to coat them; add all of the other ingredients. Marinade for 1 hour. Pre-heat the oven to 200°C/400°F/Gas 6. Transfer the potatoes to a roasting tin and roast in the pre-heated oven for 40–60 minutes until well browned and crisp.

Peas à la française
Serves 6–8

1½ lb (600 g) frozen peas or petit pois
handful of lettuce leaves, finely shredded
few spring onions or shallots, finely chopped
knob of butter
sprig of mint
sprig of parsley
1 tablespoon (15 ml) sugar
melted butter to serve

Mix all the ingredients except the melted butter together and boil, steam or microwave until tender. Drain, remove the mint and parsley, and serve coated in the melted butter.

Creamed leeks
Serves 6–8

  2 lb (800 g) leeks, sliced
  2 tablespoons (30 ml) olive oil
  2 oz (50 g) butter
  5 fl oz (125 ml) crème fraîche
  salt and pepper

Fry the leeks in the oil and butter until just starting to colour. Mix in the crème fraîche and heat through. Season well before serving.

CREAMED LEEKS WITH HORSERADISH
I sometimes make this with 1–2 tablespoons of creamed horseradish, which I add with the crème fraîche. It gives it an extra 'bite'.

Raspberry soufflé
Serves 8

This is another yummy family favourite which is also very suitable for posher entertaining occasions. If I can be bothered I sometimes wait until it is frozen and then scoop out some of the middle, fill it with fresh fruit and plug with the frozen soufflé before returning it to the freezer for a while.

1½ lb (600 g) mixed raspberries and redcurrants
10 oz (250 g) caster sugar
juice of ½ a lemon
4 egg whites
1 pint (500 ml) double cream
whipping cream to decorate

Reserve 4 oz (100 g) of the fruit to decorate the soufflé. Purée the rest (or sieve if you dislike the raspberry pips) and mix with 2 oz (50 g) of the caster sugar and the lemon juice. (For a really special occasion, I may add a little brandy at this point.) Beat the egg whites and the remaining sugar (8 oz/200 g) until they form soft peaks (you will get a lighter result if you do this in a bowl over simmering water). Lightly beat the double cream until it is just thickening. Now fold together the fruit purée, egg whites and cream. Pour into a 3 pint (1.5 litre) soufflé dish and freeze. To serve, remove the soufflé from the freezer 20–30 minutes before you wish to use it. Place the reserved fruit in the middle, and pipe whipped cream around the edges.

Curried lamb
Serves 4–6

3 large onions, thinly sliced
2 cloves garlic, crushed
1 teaspoon (5 ml) ginger purée
2 oz (50 g) concentrated cooking butter
2–3 tablespoons (30–45 ml) curry paste
1–1½ lb (400–600 g) leftover cooked lamb, cubed
8 oz (200 g) Greek yoghurt
8 oz (200 g) frozen leaf spinach, thawed
2 tablespoons (30 ml) groundnut oil

Pre-heat the oven to 180°C/350°F/Gas 4. Fry 2 of the onions with the garlic and ginger in the cooking butter until soft and brown. Add the curry paste and then start to add the lamb, transferring some of the onion and lamb to a casserole dish as the frying pan gets full. When all the meat has been coated with the curry mixture and removed to the casserole dish, add the yoghurt to the meat and stir well. Mix in the spinach. Heat through on the hob and then transfer to the pre-heated oven for 30 minutes. Before serving, fry the remaining onion in the oil until brown and serve this sprinkled over the curry.

Turkey à la King
Serves 4–6

8 oz (200 g) mushrooms, quartered
1 green pepper, diced
1 red pepper, diced
1 tablespoon (15 ml) oil
knob of butter
1 tablespoon (15 ml) plain flour
10 fl oz (250 ml) milk
dash of Tabasco
1 lb (400 g) cooked turkey, diced
2 tablespoons (30 ml) sherry or brandy
5 fl oz (125 ml) double cream
salt and pepper

Fry the mushrooms and peppers in the oil and butter for 10 minutes, until soft and browning. Stir in the flour and cook for 1–2 minutes. Gradually add the milk, while stirring. Bring to the boil and stir until the sauce thickens. Add the Tabasco and the turkey and simmer gently for 10–15 minutes. Before serving, stir in the sherry (or brandy) and the cream. Season and heat through before serving.

Shepherd's pie
Serves 4–6

2 onions, chopped
2 carrots, chopped
3 tablespoons (45 ml) oil
1–1½ lb (400–600 g) cooked lamb, minced
2 tablespoons (30 ml) tomato purée
sprinkling of parsley
dash of Worcestershire sauce
1 teaspoon (5 ml) mustard
10–15 fl oz (250–375 ml) hot brown stock
salt and pepper
2–3 lb (800 g–1.2 kg) cooked potatoes, mashed
2 oz (50 g) butter

Pre-heat the oven to 190°C/375°F/Gas 5. Fry the onion and carrot in the oil until soft. Add the lamb, tomato purée, parsley, Worcestershire sauce, mustard and stock. Season with salt and pepper. Cook for 30 minutes or until the stock is reduced by half. Put into a large, greased ovenproof dish. Mix the potato and butter together, season and use to cover the dish. Bake in the pre-heated oven until the potato is brown.

Turkey Creole
Serves 4–6

1 onion, chopped
1 red pepper, diced
1 green pepper, diced
3 cloves garlic, crushed
3 tablespoons (45 ml) oil
16 oz (400 g) can chopped tomatoes
1 tablespoon (15 ml) tomato purée
glass of white wine
1 lb (400 g) cooked turkey, diced
dash of Tabasco

Fry the onion, peppers and garlic in the oil for 10 minutes until softened and browning. Add the tomatoes, tomato purée, white wine and cooked turkey. Season to taste with Tabasco. Bring to the boil and simmer gently for 10–15 minutes.

Gado gado (Indonesian salad)
Serves 4–6

handful of lettuce leaves, shredded
8 oz (200 g) cooked green beans
1 cucumber, cut into matchsticks
1 yellow pepper, diced
10 oz (250 g) beansprouts (optional)
6 hard-boiled eggs, shells removed, cut into sixths

Peanut sauce
6 tablespoons (90 ml) crunchy peanut butter
1 tablespoon (15 ml) lemon or lime juice
1 tablespoon (15 ml) soft dark brown sugar
2 tablespoons (30 ml) soy sauce
4 fl oz (100 ml) boiling water

Melt all the ingredients for the sauce together and simmer for a few minutes until the mixture has become smooth. Arrange the salad ingredients on individual serving dishes and drizzle with the sauce.

2 Coming of Age/ Engagement Parties

These, through their very nature, tend to be celebrations for the younger generation, and as such there tends to be an emphasis more on drink rather than food. I have to admit that I am not particularly keen on engagement parties – in my experience, many couples who have them never make it to the altar! Rather, it is the ones who have been living together and who casually remark that they have decided to get married that actually turn into happily married couples. Certainly a family dinner is appropriate, so that you can toast the future happiness of the couple and actually mark the event – but a full-blown party which involves receiving engagement presents can lead to difficult problems if someone changes their mind!

However, if your son or daughter is determined to have a party I would suggest that the menus and recipes that I give here for the coming of age party are just as suitable for an engagement do.

Coming of age is a very important event, not just for the person concerned, but for the parents. (Where did all those years go?) The big question, however, is when to actually celebrate the event – do you do it at 18 or 21? I can remember with intense dissatisfaction actually celebrating my 18th birthday at someone else's 21st birthday party, and have much more pleasant recollections of my 21st, which was spent with my family in a local restaurant where we have celebrated many family occasions.

When deciding which event is going to be the really big one, you need to bear in mind that you probably still have a modicum of control over your children at 18 (especially if they are still living at home), while by the time they are 21 you really have very little say in what they want. The average 21-year-old, though, is more mature than the 18-year-old and may actually have developed some sense of family responsibility. I would suggest that you let your children have their own type of celebration at 18 – which they will probably want to have with their friends. For a 21st, however, I think a family dinner involving relatives or a more civilized party is called for – and hopefully, if they have had their own choice of celebration for their 18th, they will be amenable to celebrating their 21st with you!

I suggest that for an 18th birthday party you follow whatever guidelines your children give you on food and drink – bearing in mind that your pocket is not a bottomless pit, and also that quite often people of this age drink more than is good for them. (Do you really want the celebration in your home?) Many local night-clubs have nights when they can be hired for a private do, and this might suit your offspring perfectly. Another option that avoids letting them have the house is hiring a hall, for example a scout hall, village hall, etc. Look in your local paper to find what is available locally. I do think that halls need 'cheering up', and you can decorate them cheaply with crêpe paper, streamers and plenty of balloons. Discos are easy to hire – but they vary a lot in price, so do shop around. The hall will usually provide tables and chairs, but check, and if necessary contact a local hire company – however basic the food you are going to provide, you will need somewhere to put it. Keep the food simple – a finger buffet is the most suitable for this type of do.

Finally, make sure you have plenty of rubbish sacks and helpers at the end of the party – it's amazing how much mess these parties can generate!

I would not be averse to holding a 21st celebration at home, as by this age you can expect a more civilized affair. That is not to say that copious amounts of alcohol will not be consumed – it is just that by this age they may have learnt how to handle it a little better!

A really good way of celebrating your 21st is with a cocktail party (this gives people the option of dressing up if this is what they want, and parties are generally more fun if they have a theme). You do need plenty of helpers. While we were at university, my friend Lucy had a cocktail party to celebrate her 21st, and we had three people behind the bar in order to keep the drinks flowing.

It is fairly easy to block off a corner of a room in order to make a bar area. Make sure that you have access to a power point, as you will want to use a blender to make up some of the drinks. Dress the corner up with crêpe paper and hang a Japanese parasol above it, to make it look like an authentic bar. It is important to have plenty of glasses and ice on hand, so make arrangements for these. You also need lots of garnishes ready prepared. After that it is very easy.

For Lucy's party we chose about five cocktails to have on offer. We drew pictures of them, listing their contents, and pinned the pictures up around the bar area. This was helpful in two ways. First, people knew what they were ordering, and second, the helpers knew what glass to put the cocktail in, what to garnish it with and what to put into the cocktail itself!

The whole event was a smashing success. The only surprise came much later. When everyone had finally retired for the night, I was woken by someone trying to climb into bed with me! I screamed for Chris (Lucy's boyfriend – now husband), who came to the rescue. It turned out that the intruder was a drunken friend who had got up in the middle of the night to visit the loo – on his return he thought he was trying to get back into bed with his wife, and was mystified as to why I wasn't allowing this! He was very embarrassed in the morning, needless to say – and his wife wasn't very impressed either!

Keep the food simple – things on sticks and items that can be eaten with the fingers, such as savoury profiteroles or cheese puffs, are ideal. The important thing is the cocktails. Making them up by the pitcher will make life much simpler.

Suggested menu
(Recipes are given in the order shown below)

Food for a finger buffet
Pâtés, etc. on canapé bases
Small sandwiches
Chicken drumsticks (Hot 'n' spicy chicken, see
    page 18)
Pork or chicken satay
Dips with crudités and tortillas or pitta bread
Pizza bites
Quiche fingers
Mini pastries (see also page 12)
Cheese borek
Savoury profiteroles
Filled vol-au-vents

Drinks
Cocktails

Other suggested recipes
Provençal tartlets
Cheese puffs
Canapés on sticks

Pork satay
Serves 8

1 lb (400 g) pork fillet, cubed
3 tablespoons (45 ml) soy sauce
2 tablespoons (30 ml) soft dark brown sugar
2 tablespoons (30 ml) lemon or lime juice
1 tablespoon (15 ml) sweet chilli sauce
2 cloves garlic, crushed
sprinkling of lemon grass

Marinade the pork in the other ingredients for 4 hours. Thread on to wooden skewers and grill under a hot grill for 3 minutes on each side or until the meat is browned on all sides. Serve with satay sauce (see below).

CHICKEN SATAY
Substitute 1 lb (400 g) chicken breast for the pork fillet.

Satay sauce
Serves 8

8 fl oz (200 ml) boiling water
4 tablespoons (60 ml) desiccated coconut
4 tablespoons (60 ml) crunchy peanut butter
4 tablespoons (60 ml) soy sauce
2 tablespoons (30 ml) soft dark brown sugar
1 tablespoon (15 ml) lemon juice
2 cloves garlic, crushed
1 teaspoon (5 ml) chilli sauce

Pour the boiling water on to the coconut and stir. Leave for 30 minutes. Now put into a small saucepan and add the rest of the ingredients. Bring to the boil, then simmer while stirring until you have a thick brown sauce.

Hummus
Serves 6–10

16 oz (400 g) can chickpeas, drained
sprinkling of cumin powder
2 cloves garlic, crushed
pinch of salt
1 tablespoon (15 ml) oil
juice of ½ a lemon
6 tablespoons (90 ml) Greek yoghurt
black pepper

Put all the ingredients into a liquidizer or blender and whizz. Serve as a dip, with toast or pitta bread.

Aubergine dip
Serves 6–10

2 aubergines, sliced
4 fl oz (100 ml) olive oil
5 fl oz (125 ml) tahini paste
sprinkling of cumin
5 fl oz (125 ml) Greek yoghurt
juice of ½ a lemon
salt and pepper
chopped fresh coriander leaves to garnish

Fry the aubergine slices, in batches, in the oil, then blend with the rest of the ingredients. Check the seasoning, adding more cumin if you like. Chill before serving.

Greek garlic dip
Serves 6–10

3 oz (75 g) fresh white breadcrumbs
4 tablespoons (60 ml) milk
6 cloves garlic, crushed
10 fl oz (250 ml) olive oil
juice of 1 lemon
salt and pepper
chopped fresh parsley to garnish

Soak the bread in the milk for 10 minutes, then squeeze out the milk. Mix the bread with the garlic to form a paste. Gradually beat in the oil, and when it starts to thicken (like a mayonnaise) add some of the lemon juice. When all the olive oil has been incorporated, season well and refrigerate overnight before serving, garnished with parsley.

Quick salsa
Serves 6–10

5 tablespoons (75 ml) chilli and tomato relish
2 tablespoons (30 ml) tomato purée
2 tablespoons (30 ml) olive oil
chilli sauce

Mix together the relish, tomato purée and olive oil. Add enough chilli sauce to achieve the heat that you like.

Guacamole
Serves 6–10

2 large ripe avocados
2 cloves garlic, crushed
juice of ½ a lemon or lime
1 teaspoon (5 ml) tomato purée
1 teaspoon (5 ml) chopped fresh coriander, or a
    pinch of ground coriander

Mash or purée the avocados, then beat in the rest of the
ingredients. Cover with clingfilm until required. To serve,
put in a bowl on a large plate and surround with niblets of
fresh vegetables and tortilla chips.

Pizza bites
Makes 30

Once you have made these I'm sure you will start to make up your own favourite toppings. This just happens to be the most popular one in our house.

> 1 packet pizza base mix
> 3 tablespoons (45 ml) tomato purée
> 1 tablespoon (15 ml) red pesto
> 8 oz (200 g) soft goat's cheese
> 6–8 sun-dried tomatoes in oil, cut into strips

Pre-heat the oven to 200°C/400°F/Gas 6. Make up the pizza dough as directed on the packet. Roll out on a floured surface, as thinly as you can. Using a 2 inch (5 cm) cutter, cut out little rounds – with re-rolling the leftovers you should get 15. Cut each round in half. Spread a little tomato purée on each half, then a touch of red pesto. Spread or crumble a little goat's cheese on each and top with a strip or two of dried tomato. Bake in the pre-heated oven for 10–15 minutes until browning. Can be served hot or cold.

Shortcrust pastry
Makes 12 oz (300 g)

> 8 oz (200 g) flour
> pinch of salt
> 5 oz (125 g) butter
> cold water

Put the flour, salt and butter into a bowl. Using your fingertips, rub the mixture between your fingers until it resembles fine breadcrumbs, then, using a few tablespoons of water, mix to a dough. Use only as much water as is needed. Rest the dough in the refrigerator for 20 minutes before using. When rolling out, touch the dough as little as possible, and use a rolling pin on a floured surface.

BAKING 'BLIND'
To use shortcrust pastry in pies and tarts, you need to bake it 'blind'. Pre-heat the oven to 190°C/375°F/Gas 5. Line an 8 inch (20 cm) flan tin with the pastry, and prick the base of the pastry all over with a fork. Put some greaseproof paper in the bottom, and weigh down with coins or ceramic beans. Cook in the pre-heated oven for 15 minutes. Remove the paper and coins before using.

Cheese 'n' onion quiche fingers
Makes about 18 fingers

12 oz (300 g) shortcrust pastry
1 lb (400 g) onions, chopped
2 tablespoons (30 ml) olive oil
4 eggs, beaten
10 fl oz (250 ml) double cream
pinch of nutmeg
1 tablespoon (15 ml) Dijon mustard
6 oz (150 g) Gruyère cheese, grated
salt and pepper

Roll out the pastry to fit a 7 × 11 inch (18 × 28 cm) baking tin. Grease the tin, lay the pastry in it, and prick well with a fork. Pre-heat the oven to 190°C/375°F/Gas 5 (if you heat another baking tray at the same time and place the baking tin on this it helps to crisp the pastry base). Fry the onions in the oil until starting to soften and brown (about 10 minutes). Now mix with the rest of the ingredients. Season and spread over the pastry base. Cook the quiche in the pre-heated oven for 25–30 minutes until brown and well risen. Leave in the tin to cool for 10 minutes, then transfer to a wire rack. When completely cool, cut into fingers.

TOMATO 'N' MUSHROOM QUICHE FINGERS
Replace the onions, nutmeg and Dijon mustard with:

8 oz (200 g) sliced mushrooms
7 oz (200 g) can tomatoes, drained and chopped
2 cloves garlic, crushed
6 sun-dried tomatoes, chopped
1 tablespoon (15 ml) tomato purée

NB: The pastry can be baked 'blind' at 200°C/400°F/Gas 7 for 15 minutes if you prefer a crispier base.

Cheese borek
Makes about 24

This is one of those recipes that looks complicated but is actually very easy. Do read the instructions a couple of times before you begin – in fact it is a good idea to practise on a strip of paper before making this for the first time. This is because filo pastry dries out very quickly, so you need to work quite fast once you start.

> 8 oz (200 g) feta cheese, crumbled
> 2 eggs, beaten
> 2 tablespoons (30 ml) fresh chopped mint
> 8 sheets filo pastry
> melted butter

Pre-heat the oven to 180°C/350°F/Gas 4. Mix together the cheese, eggs and mint. Cut a sheet of filo pastry into 3 equal lengths. Put a large teaspoon of the mixture at one end of a length and brush the pastry with butter. Take the bottom right corner of the strip between finger and thumb and fold over to the left side to make a triangle. Continue folding until you reach the top. Put on a greased baking tray, with the loose pastry underneath. Brush with melted butter. Bake in the pre-heated oven for about 15 minutes until pastry is crisp and brown.

Savoury profiteroles
Choux pastry
Makes 30–40

2½ oz (60 g) butter or soft margarine
8 fl oz (200 ml) water
4 oz (100 g) plain flour
3 eggs, beaten

Pre-heat the oven to 220°C/425°F/Gas 7. Melt the fat in the water and bring to the boil. Remove from the heat and tip all the flour in together. Return to the heat and beat the paste into a smooth ball. Allow to cool a little, then gradually beat in the eggs. Either put into a piping bag and pipe small balls on to greased baking sheets, or place in small round heaps on the baking sheets (do not over-handle pastry). This will make about 30–40 balls. Bake in the pre-heated oven for 20 minutes or until brown and well risen. Make a hole in the side of each ball, and return to the oven for 5–10 minutes to dry out completely. Place on a wire rack to cool.

CHEESE FILLED
Will fill 20

6 oz (150 g) cream cheese
1 tablespoon (15 ml) mayonnaise
1 tablespoon (15 ml) chopped fresh chives
salt and pepper

Mix together the filling ingredients and season well. Either put into a piping bag and pipe through a hole in the side of the profiterole, or split a profiterole and fill.

CRAB FILLED
Will fill 20

6 oz (150 g) can whitemeat crab
2 tablespoons (30 ml) mayonnaise
1 tablespoon (15 ml) chopped fresh parsley
salt and pepper

Mix all the filling ingredients. Split the profiteroles and fill with mixture.

Caviar cups
Makes 60

This is a very impressive way of serving vol-au-vents. It's also one of the quickest fillings that you can use. However, you will find plenty of other fillings that can be used in this book. Mushroom pâté is good topped with a sliver of gherkin. From the fillings that I have used to fill the mini pastries on page 13, you could use the cheat's coronation chicken or the ham and mushroom filling. Prawnnaise (page 162) makes a good filling, as does chicken liver pâté (page 92) – which I usually top with a slice of stuffed olive. Just make sure that you do not use too runny a mixture, and do not fill them more than a few hours in advance.

    1 packet (60) frozen cocktail vol-au-vents
    4 oz (100 g) smoked salmon pâté
    1 jar lumpfish caviar
    milk to glaze

Bake the vol-au-vent cases as directed on the packet. (Watch them carefully and don't forget to turn them, as they burn easily.) Leave to cool. When cool, put a little smoked salmon pâté in each case and top with caviar. Can be made 2–4 hours in advance.

Provençal tartlets
Makes 12–16

    8 oz (200 g) puff pastry
    4 oz (100 g) Gruyère, sliced
    4 sun-dried tomatoes, sliced
    black olives, stoned and quartered
    grated Parmesan

Pre-heat the oven to 200°C/400°F/Gas 6. Grease small canapé tart tins. Roll out the pastry and cut out rounds to fit the tins. Place in the tins and add a piece of cheese, a piece of sun-dried tomato and an olive. Sprinkle with Parmesan. Bake in the pre-heated oven for about 10 minutes, until the pastry is crisp and brown.

Cheese puffs
Makes 40–50

> 2 oz (50 g) butter
> 10 fl oz (250 ml) milk
> 4 oz (100 g) plain flour
> pinch of salt
> 3 oz (75 g) strong-flavoured cheese
> pinch of paprika
> pinch of mustard powder
> 3 eggs, beaten
> grated Parmesan cheese to garnish

Pre-heat the oven to 200°C/400°F/Gas 6. Melt the butter and milk together and bring to the boil. Remove from the heat and tip in the flour. Return to the heat and cook, stirring, until you have a ball of dough. Now add the cheese and seasonings. Beat well. Gradually beat in the egg. Put the mixture into a piping bag and pipe small balls on to a baking tray. Sprinkle with Parmesan cheese. Bake in the pre-heated oven for 20 minutes, then turn the temperature down to 180°C/350°F/Gas 4 and continue to cook for a further 10 minutes until well risen and brown. Serve hot or cold.

Cheese, onion and pineapple sticks

> fresh pineapple, cubed
> cocktail onions, drained
> Cheddar cheese, cubed
> Double Gloucester cheese, cubed
> cocktail sticks

On to each cocktail stick thread a piece of pineapple, then a cocktail onion and finally a cube of cheese. Make half with Cheddar and half with Double Gloucester.

Brie and grapes on sticks

> Brie, ripe but not runny
> seedless white grapes
> seedless black grapes
> cocktail sticks

De-rind the Brie and cut into cubes. Halve the grapes. On to each cocktail stick thread ½ a grape, then a cube of Brie, followed by the second ½ grape. Make half with white and half with black grapes.

Cocktail sausages on sticks

> baby red tomatoes, halved
> cocktail gherkins, drained
> cocktail onions, drained
> cocktail sausages, cooked
> cocktail sticks

On to each cocktail stick thread ½ a tomato, a cocktail gherkin or onion and then a sausage.

Cocktails

We love cocktails – I would advocate never marrying anyone until you have found out whether they can make your favourite cocktail!

Martini
Makes 1 pitcher (6–9 drinks)

> 1 pint (½ litre) gin
> ½ pint (¼ litre) dry vermouth
> spirals of lemon peel
> ice

You will need a 2-pint (1-litre) pitcher. Mix together the gin and vermouth in the pitcher. Chill well. Just before serving, add the lemon peel and ice.

Vodka Martini
As for Martini, but substituting vodka for the gin. Of course if you are a Bond fan you will need a large cocktail shaker, so that it can be 'shaken, not stirred'.

Freddy Fudpucker
Makes 1 pitcher (4–6 drinks)

After the humble martini this is my personal favourite.
(And Andy has got it down to a fine art!)

2 pints (1 litre) orange juice
5 fl oz (125 ml) tequila
5 fl oz (125 ml) Galliano
1 orange, sliced
ice

Mix the orange juice, tequila and Galliano in a pitcher
and chill. Before serving, stir again and add orange and
ice.

HARVEY WALLBANGER
As for Freddy Fudpucker, but substituting vodka for the
tequila.

Banana daiquiri
Makes 1 pitcher (8–10 drinks)

1 pint (500 ml) clear rum
10 fl oz (250 ml) banana-flavoured liqueur
juice from 2 lemons and 1 lime
3 tablespoons (45 ml) caster sugar
10 fl oz (250 ml) cracked ice
1 lime, sliced

Try not to make this up too far in advance – it can be kept in a freezer for a short space of time. Mix all the ingredients except the sliced lime and chill. Add the lime just before serving – do not add extra ice.

Margarita
Makes 1 pitcher (8–10 drinks)

1 pint (500 ml) tequila
10 fl oz (250 ml) Cointreau
juice of 2 lemons and 1 lime
10 fl oz (250 ml) cracked ice
1 lime, cut into wedges

Again, do not make this up too far in advance – it can be kept in the freezer for a short time. Mix all the ingredients except the lime wedges and chill. Add the lime wedges just before serving – do not add extra ice. It is customary to serve Margaritas in glasses which have had their rims dipped in lemon or lime juice and then in coarse salt.

Pina colada
Makes 1 pitcher (6–8 drinks)

2 pints (1 litre) pineapple juice
10 fl oz (250 ml) clear rum
5 fl oz (125 ml) Malibu
5 fl oz (125 ml) single cream
ice

Blend together the pineapple juice, rum, Malibu and cream. Chill. Stir well and add ice just before serving.

Singapore sling
Makes 1 pitcher (6–8 drinks)

10 fl oz (250 ml) gin
5 fl oz (125 ml) cherry brandy
juice of 1 lemon
2 pints (1 litre) soda water
slices of orange
slices of lemon
sprigs of mint
ice

Mix together the gin, cherry brandy and lemon juice. Chill. Just before serving, add the rest of the ingredients.

Screwdriver
Makes 1 pitcher (4–6 drinks)

2 pints (1 litre) orange juice
10 fl oz (250 ml) vodka
ice
1 orange, sliced

Mix the orange and vodka and chill. Just before serving add the ice and orange slices.

SALTY DOG
To make a salty dog, substitute 2 pints (1 litre) grapefruit juice for the orange juice and serve in glasses which have had the rims dipped in lemon and lime juice and then in coarse salt.

Champagne cocktails

These make an impressive cocktail to start off a special meal. You can of course cheat and use a sparkling wine – and it is completely up to you whether you then rename them 'mock' champagne cocktails.

> sugar cubes
> angostura bitters
> champagne

Put a sugar cube in the bottom of each glass. Put 1–2 drops of angostura bitters on to each sugar cube. (This can be done in advance.) Fill each glass with champagne.

3 Birthday Celebrations

Many and varied are the ways of celebrating birthdays, and, after all, who would want to celebrate their 8th, 18th and 80th birthdays in the same fashion? So what I hope to do here is give you some ideas about what might appeal to certain age groups. A word of caution – surprise celebrations. If there is any doubt in your mind as to whether a 'surprise party' would be welcomed by the recipient – don't do it. There are people in the world who truly love surprises – and there are those who hate them! Often it is the person doing the planning who would really like a surprise party – not the one it is being planned for. (Psychologists call this wish fulfilment!) So please take heed if you are thinking of giving someone a surprise, and if others keep questioning the advisability of it – maybe you are doing a little bit of wishful thinking?

Tiny tots
These parties need to be kept short and simple at this age. I would suggest that one and a half hours is ample time. Everyone should have a little something to take home with them. You may well have to entertain a parent or two as well, so be prepared with nibbles and tea (or something a little stronger if they are not driving).

5–8-year-olds
The invitation itself is very important to this age group, so try to find an appropriate one for the party. I have found that a theme goes down very well. This age group likes the chance to dress up. Some themes that have been very popular have been a spaceman party, a pink party, a monster party and a superman party!

8–11-year-olds

If you are having a party at home for this age group it should be something like a well-organised barbecue or Hallowe'en party, something with a more adult theme. Many at this age will appreciate a trip out to a venue of their choice, i.e. ice-skating or ten-pin bowling with friends, or a trip to the cinema (followed by a visit to their favourite burger bar).

12 onwards

This age group is difficult – you can only be guided by the children themselves, as they mature at very different rates. At teenage parties they will not want parents visible, but you do need to be on hand. As children get older, alcohol can be a problem – some youngsters always seem to be able to gain access to it. Teenage parties can become rowdy (or suspiciously quiet!) – try not to interfere unless absolutely necessary. Teenagers must have space and need to be given a sense of responsibility.

Mum's/Dad's birthday

This is the point where you can leave this book around for your spouse/children to get the hint! It is not always possible to be taken out for a slap-up meal on your birthday, but the next best thing is to have someone else do the cooking, giving you the chance to have a relaxing bath and pamper yourself before dinner!

Suggested Menus
(Recipes are given in the order shown below)

Tiny tots
Jelly in individual bowls
Crisps and nibbles
Sandwiches
Pinwheels
Smartie cakes
Fairy cakes
Chocolate squares
Birthday cake (iced Victoria sandwich)

Drinks
Lemonade or squash

5–8-year-olds
Jacket potatoes, baked beans and coleslaw
Beefburgers in a bun
Crisps and nibbles
Flapjacks or ice-cream
Gingerbread people
Birthday cake

Drinks
Milk shakes or ice-cream floats

Teenage parties
Vegetarian lasagne or chilli con carne
Jacket potatoes
Coleslaw
Green salad
Garlic bread
Crisps and nibbles
Black Forest gateau or ice-cream and meringues

Drinks
Iced tea
Soft drinks
Beer or lager

Mum's/Dad's birthday
Mushroom broth

Chicken in ham and cheese parcels
New potatoes or tagliatelle
Carrots with coriander and lime butter

Chocolate mousse

Drinks
White wine

Children's sandwiches

Children's sandwiches should be filled with paste-like fillings. Rounds should be cut into 4 or even 6 sandwiches. Favourite fillings include tinned fish such as tuna or sardines, cream cheese or spreads and egg mayonnaise, with the egg chopped very finely. Children are also not averse to sweet fillings. (NB: It is usual to remove the bread crusts for children's sandwiches.) Here are two popular fillings.

PEANUT BUTTER AND MARMITE SANDWICHES

Use smooth peanut butter and not too much Marmite, and mix with the margarine or butter before spreading on the bread.

MARSHMALLOW FLUFF AND BANANA SANDWICHES

Mix marshmallow fluff (this is stored by the preserves section in most supermarkets) with mashed banana and spread on buttered bread.

Pinwheels

4 slices brown bread
3 oz (75 g) cream cheese
1 tablespoon (15 ml) mayonnaise
salt and pepper

Roll out the bread and cut off the crusts. Mix together the cream cheese and mayonnaise. Season. Spread over the bread slices. Now roll each slice up tightly, wrap in clingfilm and refrigerate until needed. Just before serving, remove the clingfilm and cut into slices to serve.

Smartie cakes
Makes 12

These are a top favourite with children (and go down well with the cricket club as well).

4 oz (100 g) soft margarine
4 oz (100 g) caster sugar
4 oz (100 g) self-raising flour
2 eggs, beaten

For decoration
3 oz (75 g) icing sugar
1 tablespoon (15 ml) warm water
12 Smarties

Pre-heat the oven to 190°C/350°F/Gas 5. Beat all the cake ingredients together. Spread 12 paper cases on a baking tray and divide the mixture between them. Bake in the pre-heated oven for 15–20 minutes until golden brown. Cool on a wire rack. To decorate: blend the icing sugar and water to make water icing, spoon this over the cakes and press a Smartie on to the top of each cake. Leave to set.

Fairy cakes
Makes 12

    4 oz (100 g) soft margarine or butter
    4 oz (100 g) caster sugar
    4 oz (100 g) self-raising sugar
    2 eggs, beaten

    Buttercream
    1 oz (25 g) butter
    2 oz (50 g) icing sugar
    few drops vanilla essence
    1-2 teaspoons (5–10 ml) milk

Pre-heat the oven to 190°C/375°F/Gas 5. Beat all the cake ingredients together. Spread 12 paper cases out on a baking tray and divide the mixture between them. Bake in the pre-heated oven for about 15 minutes until the cakes are golden brown and feel 'springy' when touched. Leave on a wire rack to cool. When cool, slice off the top of each cake and cut each circle in half (these form the fairy 'wings'). Make the buttercream by creaming the butter, sugar and vanilla essence together, adding just enough milk to form a smooth paste. Put some buttercream on each cake and then place the 'wings' on top.

Chocolate squares
Makes 24

    8 oz (200 g) plain cooking chocolate
    3 oz (75 g) soft margarine or butter
    3 tablespoons (45 ml) runny honey
    12 oz (300 g) digestive biscuits, crushed
    24 Maltesers

Melt the chocolate, fat and honey. Stir in the crushed biscuits and mix thoroughly. Turn into a greased and lined 7 × 11 inch (18 × 28 cm) tin. Spacing the Maltesers equally apart, and making 4 lines of 6 Maltesers, push them down into the mixture. Leave to set and then cut into squares with a Malteser in the middle of each square.

Victoria sandwich cake
Makes 1 × 7 inch (18 cm) cake

To make a birthday cake, you can use a basic Victoria sandwich cake mixture, filling it with jam and/or butter-cream. Coat with a bought fondant icing (these are very easy to roll out). Decorate with ribbons, candles and bought decorations.

> 6 oz (150 g) soft margarine or butter
> 6 oz (150 g) caster sugar
> 3 eggs, beaten
> 6 oz (150 g) self-raising flour

> *To serve*
> jam or lemon curd
> icing sugar

Pre-heat the oven to 190°C/375°F/Gas 5. Cream together the fat and sugar. Gradually beat in the eggs, adding a little of the flour to ensure that the eggs do not curdle. Finally, fold in the remaining flour. Divide the mixture between 2 greased and lined 7 inch (18 cm) sandwich tins. Bake in the pre-heated oven for 20–30 minutes, or until they are well risen, brown, 'springy' to the touch and starting to shrink away from the sides of the tin. Turn out on to a wire rack to cool. Sandwich together with your chosen filling and sprinkle with icing sugar.

Jacket potatoes

a 6–8 oz (150–200 g) potato per person
olive oil
salt

Pre-heat the oven to 200°C/400°F/Gas 6. Rub the potatoes with oil and salt, and cook for 1–1½ hours.

Flapjacks

4 oz (100 g) butter
4 oz (100 g) soft dark brown sugar
1 tablespoon (15 ml) golden syrup
6 oz (150 g) porridge oats

Pre-heat the oven to 180°C/350°F/Gas 4. Put the butter, sugar and syrup in a saucepan and heat gently until the mixture melts. Remove from the heat and stir in the oats. Mix well, then press into a greased 7 × 11 inch (18 × 28 cm) baking tin. Cook in the pre-heated oven for 25–30 minutes. Mark into portions while still hot, but leave in the tin to cool.

Gingerbread people
Makes 12

1 oz (25 g) soft margarine
2 oz (50 g) soft dark brown sugar
2 tablespoons (30 ml) golden syrup
4 oz (100 g) plain flour
pinch of ground ginger
1 teaspoon (5 ml) milk
½ teaspoon (2.5 ml) bicarbonate of soda

Pre-heat the oven to 160°C/325°F/Gas 3. Melt the margarine, sugar and syrup, then mix with all the other ingredients to form a dough. Put in a plastic bag and chill for 30 minutes. Roll out on a floured surface and use gingerbread cutters to cut out your people. Place on a greased baking tray. Bake in the pre-heated oven for 10–15 minutes, or until firm to the touch. Place on a wire rack to cool. If you wish you can decorate them with coloured marzipan for clothes or glacé icing to pipe on faces, buttons, etc.

Vegetarian lasagne
Serves 8

2 onions, chopped
4 cloves garlic, crushed
4 tablespoons (60 ml) olive oil
1 lb (400 g) browncap mushrooms, chopped
1 aubergine, diced
3 shredded basil leaves
1 glass of red wine
14 oz (400 g) can chopped tomatoes
6 sun-dried tomatoes in oil, chopped
3 tablespoons (45 ml) tomato purée
15 fl oz (375 ml) white sauce, made with 1 oz (25 g)
   flour and 1 oz (25 g) butter
3 tablespoons (45 ml) double cream
6 oz (150 g) lasagne
12 oz (300 g) cheese, grated

Pre-heat the oven to 190°C/375°F/Gas 5. Fry the onion and garlic in half of the oil until soft and browning. Transfer them to a casserole dish. Now fry the mushrooms in the rest of the oil for 5 minutes, and transfer them to the dish. Fry the aubergines until brown and add to the casserole dish with the basil, wine, canned and sun-dried tomatoes, and purée. Bring to the boil, cover, and simmer for 10–15 minutes until reduced to a thick sauce. Layer into a lasagne dish the sauce, lasagne sheets, white sauce, cream and cheese. Cook in the pre-heated oven for 40–50 minutes, until well browned on top.

Chilli con carne
Serves 8–10

- 3 onions, chopped
- 3 cloves garlic, crushed
- 1 red pepper, diced
- 1 green pepper, diced
- 4 tablespoons (60 ml) olive oil
- 2 lb (800 g) braising steak, cubed
- 1 lb (400 g) lean minced beef
- 2 × 16 oz (2 × 400 g) cans chopped tomatoes
- 2 tablespoons (30 ml) tomato purée
- 1 tablespoon (15 ml) cane molasses or treacle
- 1 bay leaf
- 2 teaspoons (10 ml) cumin
- 2 teaspoons (10 ml) oregano
- 1 teaspoon (5 ml) cayenne pepper
- 2–3 tablespoons (30–45 ml) 'lazy' chilli
- 2 × 14 oz (2 × 400 g) cans red kidney beans, drained

Pre-heat the oven to 170°C/325°F/Gas 3. In batches, fry the onions, garlic, peppers, braising steak and mince in the oil – just brown and then add to a casserole dish. Add all the other ingredients except the kidney beans. Bring to the boil, transfer to the pre-heated oven, and cook for 3 hours. 30 minutes before the end of cooking, add the kidney beans.

Garlic bread

1 French baguette
4 oz (100 g) softened butter
2 cloves garlic, crushed
1 tablespoon (15 ml) chopped fresh parsley

Pre-heat the oven to 160°C/325°F/Gas 3. Cut the bread into thick slices, without completely separating each slice. Cream together the butter, garlic and parsley. Spread some of the mixture on each sliced side of bread. Wrap bread loosely in foil and bake in the pre-heated oven for 15 minutes. Raise the oven temperature to 220°C/425°F/Gas 7 and fold the foil back from the bread. Cook for a further 5–10 minutes until crisp.

Herby Italian bread

1 pizza base
1 oz (25 g) softened butter
1 clove garlic, crushed
1 tablespoon (15 ml) chopped fresh parsley

Pre-heat the oven to 220°C/425°F/Gas 7. Mix together the butter, garlic and parsley and spread over the pizza base. Place on a baking tray and cook in the pre-heated oven for 10 minutes.

Chocolate cake
Makes a 7 inch (18 cm) cake

All in one cakes made with oil became popular in the seventies – although I never went over to this method for most of my cake recipes, preferring to use soft margarine on the whole. For some reason the method does lend itself to chocolate cake. This is a delicious cake that I have made on many occasions. I have also given an alternative which I use if I am making a cake for dessert – when I prefer a cake which is moister and with an even more intense flavour.

6 oz (150 g) self-raising flour
1 teaspoon (5 ml) baking powder
3 tablespoons (45 ml) cocoa
5 oz (125 g) caster sugar
5 fl oz (125 ml) sunflower oil
5 fl oz (125 ml) milk
2 eggs, separated

Coffee buttercream
3 oz (75 g) butter, softened
6 oz (150 g) icing sugar
1 tablespoon (15 ml) coffee essence

Pre-heat the oven to 170°C/325°F/Gas 3. Whisk together all the ingredients for the cake except the egg-whites. Whisk the egg-whites until stiff and fold into the cake mixture. Pour into 2 greased and lined 7 inch (18 cm) cake tins. Bake in the pre-heated oven for 35–45 minutes until risen and brown. Turn out on to a wire rack. When cool, sandwich together with coffee buttercream, made by creaming all the buttercream ingredients together (add a little milk, if the cream is too stiff). Sprinkle the top of the cake with icing sugar.

BLACK FOREST GATEAU

Use this recipe, adding another tablespoon of cocoa and substituting 1 oz (25 g) of the sugar with 1 dessertspoon (10 ml) black treacle. This makes a darker, moister cake. Sandwich together with black cherry jam, and decorate the top with whipped cream, black cherries and mini chocolate logs.

Coffee caramel meringues
Makes 8 shells or 16 biscuits

    2 egg whites
    4 oz (100 g) light brown muscovado sugar
    2 teaspoons (10 ml) Camp coffee essence

Pre-heat the oven to 120°C/250°F/Gas ½. Beat the egg-whites until stiff (so that you can hold the bowl upside down!). Gradually beat in half the sugar, until the mixture has regained its stiffness. Fold in the rest of the sugar and then the coffee. Line 2 baking trays with baking parchment and put the meringue mixture into a piping bag. Pipe out 8 shells or 16 small lengths. Bake in the pre-heated oven for 2 hours until crisp and dry. Remove from the paper immediately and cool on a wire rack.

ELDERFLOWER MERINGUES

Substitute caster sugar for the muscovado, and elder-flower cordial for the Camp coffee.

NB: Instead of piping the shells, you can place the meringue in small heaps on the baking trays.

Mushroom broth
Serves 4

15 fl oz (375 ml) dark vegetable stock, made with 1
   oz (25 g) dried porcini mushrooms and 15 fl oz
   (375 ml) of boiling water
1 onion, finely chopped
1 clove garlic, crushed
3 tablespoons (45 ml) olive oil
1 teaspoon (5 ml) chopped thyme
1 teaspoon (5 ml) chopped marjoram
8 oz (200 g) chestnut mushrooms, finely chopped
1 glass of red wine
2 tablespoons (30 ml) tomato purée
1 tablespoon (15 ml) chopped fresh parsley
salt and pepper
squeeze of lemon juice

Start by soaking the porcini mushrooms in the boiling
water to make the vegetable stock. Fry the onion and
garlic in the oil for 5 minutes until soft. Add the herbs and
mushrooms, and cook for a further 5 minutes. Add the
rest of the ingredients. Bring to the boil, cover and
simmer for 30 minutes.

Chicken in ham and cheese parcels
Serves 4

    4 large slices of Parma ham
    4 boneless chicken breasts, skinned
    4 oz (100 g) Gruyère cheese, grated
    salt and pepper
    knob of butter
    4 tablespoons (60 ml) chicken stock
    4 tablespoons (60 ml) dry white vermouth or wine
    1 tablespoon (15 ml) chopped fresh parsley

Pre-heat the oven to 180°C/350°F/Gas 4. Lay out the Parma ham and place a chicken breast on each slice. Sprinkle with a little cheese and season. Roll up the ham with the cheese and chicken inside and secure with cocktail sticks. Melt the butter in a frying pan and brown the rolls on all sides. Pour the stock and vermouth into the pan and bring to the boil. Transfer to a casserole dish. Sprinkle with the remaining cheese and the parsley and cook in the pre-heated oven for 25–30 minutes.

Flavoured butters

We are butter fanatics in our family. Although I will use a soft margarine for baking with, for most dishes I much prefer the taste of butter. Certainly I can think of no better accompaniment to vegetables than butter – unless it is a flavoured one! These are our favourites (although I wouldn't serve them all at one meal!).

Broccoli with anchovy butter
Serves 4

> 8 anchovy fillets
> 4 oz (100 g) unsalted butter, softened
> pinch paprika
> 1 lb (400 g) broccoli

Beat the anchovies and butter together, and sprinkle with the paprika. Boil, steam or microwave the broccoli until tender. Serve hot, with the anchovy butter melting over the broccoli.

Carrots with coriander and lime butter
Serves 4

> 1 tablespoon (15 ml) fresh chopped coriander
> grated rind of 1 lime
> 4 oz (100 g) butter, softened
> black pepper
> 1 lb (400 g) carrots, cut into matchsticks

Mix together the coriander, lime and butter, and season with black pepper. Boil, steam or microwave the carrots. Serve hot with the coriander and lime butter.

Courgettes with basil and pepper butter
Serves 4

1 red pepper, diced
1 tablespoon (15 ml) fresh chopped basil
4 oz (100 g) butter, softened
black pepper
1 lb (400 g) courgettes, cut into matchsticks

Blend or purée the red pepper, basil and butter, and season with black pepper. Steam or microwave the courgettes. Serve hot with the basil and pepper butter.

Chocolate mousse
Serves 4

8 oz (200 g) dark cooking chocolate
4 tablespoons (60 ml) brandy
2 oz (50 g) unsalted butter
4 eggs, separated, or 2 eggs and 5 fl oz (125 ml)
   double cream

Melt the chocolate with the brandy and butter. Cool slightly before adding the egg yolks and stirring in. Whisk the egg whites and cream (if using) separately. The egg whites must be whipped until stiff, the cream until it has reached the soft peak stage. Fold the egg whites and cream into the mousse and stir well. Chill.

Children's drinks

Although these drinks are supposed to be for children, I have to admit that I am addicted to ice-cream and soda floats. If he was around on our return from school, my father used to make these for us in very hot weather, and they are very refreshing. I specifically bought some long-handled spoons just for these!

Milk shakes

For each drink put into a blender ½ a banana or a few ounces of soft fruit, a scoop of ice-cream, and a glass of milk. Whizz together and serve in a long glass with a straw.

Ice-cream floats

Into a long glass put a scoop of ice-cream. Top up with Coca Cola or cream soda (carefully, as it fizzes alarmingly). Serve with a long-handled spoon and a straw.

4 Family Barbecues

What optimists we are! The slightest sniff of spring in the air and out comes the trusty (often rusty) barbecue. Often, however, what seemed like a good idea earlier in the day when we were basking in the sun doesn't seem so good when the sun has gone down . . . and we are still waiting for the charcoal to be hot enough to barbecue on . . . Oh, well!

In the heat of the summer though, it can be very different. The family barbecue has become very popular and is fast replacing the traditional Sunday lunch. I think there are two reasons for this. First, it does get the lady of the house out of cooking, as traditionally the barbecue is the one culinary area

that can be left to the men. Second, it is a very pleasant way of spending a long, lazy Sunday afternoon, and its informality lends itself well to multi-generational affairs.

Here are the tips that we have picked up over the years.

1 Always be prepared for the weather's unpredictability. We have on many occasions had to have someone holding an umbrella over the barbecue and cook – on some occasions you may have to abandon the barbecue and retire defeated to the house.
2 Make sure you have plenty of charcoal and fire-lighters to get the fire going, and that it is lit in good time. Many is the time that the barbecue has been roaring away just as we were retiring to bed!
3 Do allow plenty of food. There is something about being out in the open air and the heavenly smell of food being barbecued that greatly increases the appetite.
4 Make sure that you have a repellent for flying insects – and that if barbecuing in the evening you will have enough light to see what you are doing.

As I write this, summer is fast approaching and although outside it is grey and the outlook bleak, just thinking about the coming summer months is making my mouth water – there really is something about the smell of the charcoal and the sizzling of the meat on the barbecue that gets the taste buds going . . .

Suggested menu
(Recipes are given in the order shown below)

Barbecue
Tandoori drumsticks
Spare ribs (marinated in barbecue sauce)
Barbecued vegetables
Fish kebabs
Selection of salads
Garlic bread (see page 63)

Lemon meringue pie
Ice cream served in brandy snap baskets

Other suggested recipes
Lamburgers
Pork and apple burgers
Barbecued lamb
Lamb kebabs
Vegetable kebabs
Barbecued prawns
Barbecued sardines
Barbecued bass

Tandoori drumsticks
Serves 10 (or 20 as part of a buffet)

20 chicken drumsticks, skinned
10 fl oz (250 ml) natural yoghurt
3 tablespoons (45 ml) white wine vinegar
1 tablespoon (15 ml) paprika
1 tablespoon (15 ml) coriander
1 tablespoon (15 ml) cumin
1 tablespoon (15 ml) ginger purée
8 cloves garlic, crushed
few drops of red food colouring (optional)

Slash each chicken drumstick 2 or 3 times. Mix the rest of the ingredients to make a marinade and pour over the chicken. Leave for at least 4 hours. Cook over a medium hot heat on the barbecue for 15–25 minutes, turning frequently.

Spare ribs
Serves 10 (or 20 as part of a buffet)

4 lb (1.6 kg) pork spare ribs

Sauce
4 tablespoons (60 ml) runny honey
4 tablespoons (60 ml) soy sauce
1 tablespoon (15 ml) tomato purée
5 fl oz (125 ml) tomato ketchup
5 fl oz (125 ml) freshly squeezed orange juice
4 cloves garlic, crushed
dash of chilli sauce

Mix all the sauce ingredients together and pour over the spare ribs. Marinade for at least 4 hours. Cook over a medium hot barbecue for 20–40 minutes. Turn once during cooking and baste with marinade.

BARBECUE SAUCE
This sauce can also be used for bought beefburgers or sausages. Again, marinade in the ingredients and then barbecue over a medium-hot heat, basting with marinade.

Barbecued vegetables

AUBERGINES
Cut into thick slices, coat with oil and cook for 8–10 minutes.

CORN-ON-THE-COB
Rub with oil and salt, and cook for 8–12 minutes.

COURGETTES
Cut into large slices diagonally. Brush with oil and cook for 5–6 minutes.

PEPPERS
Cut each pepper into 3 or 4 slices. Coat with oil and cook for 8–10 minutes.

TOMATOES
Use beef tomatoes and cut into 3 or 4 slices. Coat with oil and sprinkle with herbs. Cook for 1 minute on each side.

Fish kebabs
Serves 10 (or 20 as part of a buffet)

4 lb (1.6 kg) firm-fleshed white fish
40 small cherry tomatoes
juice of 2 lemons
2 cloves garlic, crushed
2 tablespoons (30 ml) sherry
4 fl oz (100 ml) olive oil
salt and pepper

Cube the fish and marinade in the lemon juice, garlic, sherry, oil and seasoning for at least 2 hours. Thread on to skewers with the tomatoes and cook over a high heat (basting with marinade) for 10 minutes, turning to cook all sides.

Lemon meringue pie
Serves 6–8

> 12 oz (300 g) shortcrust pastry
> 3 tablespoons (45 ml) cornflour
> 5 fl oz (125 ml) water
> grated rind and juice of 3 lemons
> 10 oz (250 g) caster sugar
> 3 eggs, separated

Pre-heat the oven to 220°C/425°F/Gas 7. Roll out the pastry to fit an 8 inch (20 cm) pie dish. Bake 'blind' in the pre-heated oven for 15 minutes. Blend together the cornflour and water, and put into a small saucepan with the lemon rind and juice and 4 oz (100 g) sugar. When the sugar has dissolved, leave to cool slightly. Beat the egg-yolks and add to the lemon mixture. Spoon into the pastry case. Beat the egg white with half the remaining sugar. When stiff, fold in the remaining sugar and pile on top of the lemon. Bake in the oven for 10–15 minutes until the meringue is crisp and lightly browned.

LIME MERINGUE PIE
Replace the lemons with 3 limes.

ORANGE MERINGUE PIE
Replace the lemons with 3 oranges. Reduce the amount of sugar dissolved in the filling to 3 oz (75 g).

Brandy snap baskets
Makes 8

You can buy these at a number of supermarkets now – so I admit that I am making them less often. However, it is still a useful recipe to know because sometimes you want to make larger baskets than those you can buy – and of course you can also roll up the circles to make brandy snaps! I use these baskets quite a lot when entertaining, as I like to serve ice-cream and sorbets in them – sometimes accompanied by fudge sauce or fruit purées.

My all-time favourite dessert in a restaurant is a brandy snap basket filled with orange and pernod sorbet and topped with a cage of spun sugar! This is the way that Glovers, the restaurant close to where my mother lives, serves its sorbets. We have used this particular restaurant for various family celebrations – going right back to my twenty-first birthday. It's when a restaurant comes up with dishes like this that I never begrudge the money spent on the meal – and when good food is accompanied by attentive service and congenial surroundings, you have the perfect ingredients for a wonderful evening, which is something we have always had at this, our favourite restaurant. If only there were more like it!

>   2 oz (50 g) caster sugar
>   2 oz (50 g) butter
>   2 tablespoons (30 ml) golden syrup
>   2 oz (50 g) plain flour
>   1 tablespoon (15 ml) lemon juice
>   pinch of ground ginger

Pre-heat the oven to 180°C/350°F/Gas 4. Gently melt the sugar, butter and syrup. Stir in the rest of ingredients. Line a baking sheet with baking parchment. Make 4 baskets at a time: place 4 large teaspoons of the mixture onto the parchment, giving each plenty of room to expand. Bake in the pre-heated oven for about 10 minutes, or until an even golden brown. Meanwhile lightly grease 4 objects which you can use to mould the baskets – I suggest oranges, the bottom of jam jars or the outside of small brioche tins. When the baskets are cooked, get your moulds ready and gently ease the brandy snap mixture off the tray – if too hot to handle leave for about 1 minute but do not let them get brittle. Place each mixture over a mould and shape into a basket. (If the brandy snaps start to harden, put them back into the oven for a minute and soften them again.) Allow the baskets to cool, and when hard, store in an airtight container until needed. You can make these a day in advance if you wish.

Lamburgers
Serves 8

If you have problems with your burgers disintegrating when you cook them, try mixing some egg-yolk into the mixture when you make them. It does make them easier to handle.

1½ lb (600 g) minced lamb
3 cloves garlic, crushed
3 tablespoons (45 ml) chopped fresh parsley
1 tablespoon (15 ml) chopped fresh mint
salt and pepper

To serve
8 burger buns

Mix all the burger ingredients together and with damp hands divide into 8 equal portions. Roll into balls and then flatten into burger shapes. Put on to a plate, keeping each one separate from its neighbours with clingfilm between each one, and chill. Cook on the barbecue until both sides are really brown and the meat is cooked, which will take about 12 minutes depending on the heat of your barbecue. Serve in burger buns with your chosen relish.

Pork and apple burgers
Serves 8

1½ lb (600 g) minced pork
2 cloves garlic, crushed
2 teaspoons (10 ml) Worcestershire sauce
1 apple, cored, peeled and grated finely
1 tablespoon (15 ml) chopped chives
salt and pepper

To serve
8 burger buns

Mix all the burger ingredients together with damp hands. Divide into 8 portions, roll into balls and flatten. Put on to a plate, keeping them apart with clingfilm, and chill. Cook on the barbecue, turning once, until they brown on both sides and are well cooked (about 15 minutes). Serve in burger buns.

Barbecued lamb
Serves 10 (or 20 as part of a buffet)

20 rib lamb chops
olive oil
4 cloves garlic, crushed
4 sprigs of rosemary, chopped
salt and pepper

Marinade the chops overnight in the other ingredients. Cook on a charcoal barbecue until well done on both sides (about 15–20 minutes). Brush with marinade both before and during cooking to ensure the chops are moist.

Lamb kebabs
Serves 10 (or 20 as part of a buffet)

2 lb (800 g) lean lamb, cubed
3 green peppers, cubed
4 fl oz (100 ml) soy sauce
4 fl oz (100 ml) olive oil
2 tablespoons (30 ml) tarragon vinegar
2 cloves garlic, crushed
2 tablespoons (30 ml) chopped fresh chives
2 tablespoons (30 ml) chopped fresh mint
salt and pepper

Marinade the lamb and peppers in the other ingredients for at least 4 hours. Thread on to skewers and cook over a medium hot heat for 15–25 minutes, brushing with the marinade and turning to cook all sides.

Vegetable kebabs
Serves 10 (or 20 as part of a buffet)

2 red peppers, diced
2 green peppers, diced
2 yellow peppers, diced
2 aubergines, diced
40 cherry tomatoes
40 button mushrooms
4 fl oz (100 ml) olive oil
4 fl oz (100 ml) orange juice
4 cloves garlic, crushed
4 tablespoons (60 ml) soy sauce
salt and pepper

Thread the assorted vegetables on to skewers. Shake the remaining ingredients together and brush over the kebabs. Cook the vegetables over a medium hot heat for 10 minutes, turning and basting them as they cook.

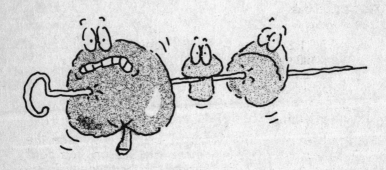

Barbecued prawns
Serves 10 (or 20 as part of a buffet)

> 2 lb (800 g) shell-on prawns
> 3 tablespoons (45 ml) sea salt
> large pinches of paprika, oregano and cumin

You need a large frying pan or skillet to cook these – or a large foil tin with holes pricked in it. Heat the pan first, then add the sea salt and spices. When the salt starts to pop, add the prawns and cook for 6–8 minutes, stirring well.

Barbecued sardines

> sardines (2–4 per person)
> olive oil
> fresh thyme
> salt and pepper

Brush the sardines with oil and sprinkle with thyme. Season well. Cook over a high heat for about 4 minutes on each side.

Barbecued bass
Serves 4–6

> 3–4 lb (1.2–1.6 kg) sea bass, cleaned
> 4 oz (100 g) garlic butter
> salt and pepper
> 1 glass of white wine
> grated rind and juice of 1 lemon
> chopped fresh herbs, dill or thyme

Put the bass on a large sheet of foil. Slice or cube the garlic butter and place inside the fish. Season, and pour the wine and lemon juice over the fish. Sprinkle with the grated rind and herbs. Wrap the fish loosely with the foil so that the juices cannot escape. Barbecue for 45–55 minutes until the flesh flakes and the fish is cooked.

5 Weddings

This is an area where different people will have different ideas about what they want. If either the bride or groom is going to be responsible for most of the catering, they will obviously need to choose dishes where most of the work can be done in advance. They will also need a number of helpers on the day who know what they are expected to do, and of course the helpers will also have to be around to do the clearing up after the event (a job which should never be underestimated).

The beauty of catering for your own wedding is that you will be able to keep the cost down considerably. Even quite a simple spread for a reasonable number of guests can be inordinately expensive when done by a caterer – after all, at the end of the day if they can't make a reasonable profit from the

event it isn't worth their while. So if you need to save on costs this is one area where corners can be cut without a detrimental effect on the final result. As an example, let me give you the menu for my own wedding – which we could never have afforded if a caterer had been responsible for the food.

Cas and Andy's wedding breakfast
Assorted canapés

Melon-filled orange baskets with Cointreau

Mayonnaise dip with crab claws and head-on prawns
Smoked salmon platter
Lobster mayonnaise
Prawnnaise (see page 162)

Cold beef Stroganoff
Coronation chicken
Roasted glazed ham (see page 163)
Selection of quiches and salads

Selection of desserts and cheeses

The food was delicious and yet it was not a difficult menu to produce.

The venue for your wedding breakfast will of course be dependent on your purse and the number of guests that you will have. We were lucky in being able to hire a large room and hall in an old grange, so we had somewhere to welcome our guests before leading them through to a seated buffet.

Many historic buildings are now able to offer their facilities, and these are the ideal setting for a romantic wedding. Narrow boats can be hired, for cruising down canals, and local restaurants often have private rooms available. A cheaper option is to hire a local hall – when decorated with crêpe paper, ribbons and balloons, these can look very effective. Throughout the country there are plenty of companies which can supply all the necessary cutlery, crockery, etc. Waiting staff can be hired from agencies.

If you are lucky enough to have a reasonable-sized house you may be able to cope with your guests at home – although this will usually have to be a standing-up affair, unless you are talking about a very small number of guests.

If you are confident about the weather I would suggest you consider a rather grand picnic in the grounds of a lovely house – but don't forget to get permission, as there is often a small fee to pay.

Consider all your options before deciding – there may well be a local attraction that would provide the perfect setting for your dream reception.

Suggested menus
(Recipes are given in the order shown below)

Fork buffet
Canapés

Avocados filled with prawnnaise

Cold beef Stroganoff and/or coronation chicken
Cold meat platter
Selection of salads

Selection of desserts and cheeses
Wedding cake (see page 187)

Drinks
Wine and champagne or sparkling wine for toasts
Soft drinks

Vegetarian wedding breakfast
Canapés

Mixed platters of dips and crudités (see pages 34-6),
cheese borek (see page 40), quiche fingers (see page
39)

Mushroom and egg plait (see page 17)
Selection of salads

Selection of desserts and cheeses
Wedding cake (see page 187)

Drinks
Wine and champagne or sparkling wine for toasts
Soft drinks

Canapé bases

I often like to serve canapés at the beginning of a meal, and there are many recipes in this book that are suitable for spreading on or filling canapé bases. Here are the bases that I most commonly use. Canapés should never be made too far in advance of when you want to serve them, as they start to lose their crispness. As well as fillings such as pâté you can also put soft cheeses on canapé bases – if you have some bases ready made, nothing could be quicker or easier to make. Decorate with slices of gherkin or olives, lump-fish caviar or tiny pieces of smoked meats or fruits or vegetables. Fresh herbs can also be used to decorate canapés.

Croûtes
Makes 20–30

> French loaf
> olive oil
> garlic cloves, crushed

Pre-heat the oven to 180°C/350°F/Gas 4. Slice the French loaf into thin rounds. Mix together some olive oil and garlic. Brush the slices on both sides with the garlicky oil. Place on a baking sheet and bake in the pre-heated oven for 15–20 minutes or until they are crisp and brown. Watch carefully, as they burn easily! They can be stored for 1–2 weeks in an airtight tin.

Tartlets
Makes 8–12

    4 oz (100 g) shortcrust pastry

Pre-heat the oven to 190°C/375°F/Gas 5. Roll out the pastry on a floured surface. Using a pastry cutter, cut out rounds and use to line small tartlet or canapé tins. Prick the bases with a fork. Bake in the pre-heated oven for 10–15 minutes until crisp and brown. Transfer to a wire rack and cool. Again, these can be stored for 5–7 days in an airtight container.

Bread cases

    sliced white bread
    butter
    cloves garlic, crushed
    salt and pepper

Pre-heat the oven to 180°C/350°F/Gas 4. Roll out the bread as thinly as possible. Using a pastry cutter, cut out rounds, brush each side with a mixture of butter and garlic, and use these to line small tartlet or canapé tins. Season. Bake in the pre-heated oven for 10–15 minutes until crisp and brown. Cool on a wire rack and store in an airtight container (they will stay fresh for 1–2 weeks).

Kipper pâté

    12 oz (300 g) cooked kipper fillets, skinned
    4 oz (100 g) curd cheese
    juice of 1 lemon
    2 tablespoons (30 ml) white wine
    4 oz (100 g) butter, softened
    sprinkling of fresh parsley
    black pepper

Blend all the ingredients together and chill. This, and the following pâté recipes, will serve 4–6 as a starter, 6–10 as part of a buffet and are enough to spread on 20–30 canapés.

Smoked trout with horseradish pâté

12 oz (300 g) smoked trout fillets, skinned
5 oz (125 g) cream cheese
3 spring onions, chopped
1 tablespoon (15 ml) creamed horseradish
juice of 1 lemon
salt and pepper

Blend all the ingredients together and chill.

Mushroom pâté

This is a very versatile recipe that I have used on many occasions. I first developed it when I was planning a twelve-course dinner to celebrate both New Year's Eve and my friend Sue's birthday (which falls on New Year's Day). As we were catering for vegetarians I needed something which I could use for a main course. I chose this pâté and served it 'en croûte' with a Madeira sauce. It was a great success and I have since used it in many different combinations. It can be used to fill cocktail vol-au-vents, to spread on canapé bases, or for mushroom and egg plait.

1 lb (400 g) chestnut mushrooms, chopped
1 onion, chopped
4 oz (100 g) butter, melted
6 tablespoons (90 ml) medium dry sherry
salt and pepper

Gently fry the mushrooms and onion in half of the butter until soft. Add the sherry and continue to cook until all the liquid has evaporated. Blend with the rest of the butter and season well. Leave to cool before using.

Chicken liver pâté

2 small onions, chopped
4 cloves garlic, crushed
4 oz (100 g) butter
2 lb (800 g) chicken livers, chopped
2 tablespoons (30 ml) tomato purée
2 tablespoons (30 ml) brandy
4 fl oz (100 ml) red wine
1 tablespoon (15 ml) double cream
salt and pepper
chopped fresh tarragon

Fry the onion and garlic in the butter for 4 minutes. Stir in the chicken livers and cook for 5 minutes. Add the tomato purée, brandy and red wine and cook for a further 5 minutes. Blend or purée with the cream, season well and add the tarragon. Cool and chill before serving.

Cold beef Stroganoff
Serves 10 (or 20 as part of a buffet)

This was one of the dishes that I made for my wedding. Yes, it is expensive. So you can only indulge on very special occasions – but it is also very easy to make and absolutely delicious. Its only drawback is that you can't really make it too far in advance – it should really be made on the day that you are going to serve it.

    3 lb (1.2 kg) rump steak, cut into strips
    4 tablespoons (60 ml) olive oil
    2 onions, sliced
    2 garlic cloves, crushed
    10 fl oz (250 ml) mayonnaise
    5 fl oz (125 ml) double cream, lightly whipped
    2 tablespoons (30 ml) mango chutney
    1 tablespoon (15 ml) Worcester sauce
    1 tablespoon (15 ml) French mustard
    1 tablespoon (15 ml) tomato purée
    1 tablespoon (15 ml) lemon juice
    salt and pepper

Fry the steak in the oil for a few minutes until browned on all sides. Remove to a mixing bowl. Fry the onion and garlic until soft and starting to colour. Mix in with the beef. Add the rest of the ingredients and stir well. Leave to cool. Refrigerate for at least 3 hours.

Coronation chicken
Serves 30 as part of a buffet

This is a very easy recipe to make and it is very useful, as the preparation is all done in advance. Do be warned, however, that it is time-consuming. We recently used this as part of the main course at my mother's 60th birthday bash. Two days before the event I and my mother spent a merry afternoon cooking, cooling and shredding the chickens and making up the sauce – we also quaffed a fair amount of wine!

> 4 × 3.5 lb (1.4 kg) corn-fed chickens
> 2 carrots, sliced
> 1 onion, sliced
> 4 bay leaves
> 20 black peppercorns
> 1 lb (400 g) onion, chopped
> 4 oz (100 g) butter
> 20 no-soak dried apricots, chopped
> 1 sachet of saffron
> grated rind of 4 lemons
> 8 tablespoons (120 ml) runny honey
> 8 oz (200 g) jar medium curry paste
> 1 litre dry white wine
> 1 pint (500 ml) mayonnaise
> 5 fl oz (125 ml) double cream
> watercress to serve

Place the chickens in large saucepans with boiling water. Divide the carrots, sliced onion, bay leaves and peppercorns between the chickens. Cover the pans, bring to the boil and then simmer for 1–1¼ hours until the chickens are cooked. (If pricked the juices will run clear.) Cool in the liquid. When cool, remove the skin and bones and cut the chicken into bite-size pieces. Refrigerate.

To make the sauce, cook the chopped onion in the butter until soft. Add the apricots, saffron, lemon rind, honey, curry paste and wine. Simmer uncovered for 1 hour until the mixture has thickened and reduced. Cool and refrigerate. Up to this stage, the recipe can be done 2 days before the event. A few hours before serving, mix the sauce with the mayonnaise and cream, then stir in the chicken. Serve on a bed of watercress.

Strawberry cream
Serves 6–8

1½ lb (600 g) strawberries
4 tablespoons (60 ml) Grand Marnier
10 fl oz (250 ml) whipping cream
1 teaspoon (5 ml) vanilla essence
2 sachets gelatine (1 oz/25 g)
10 fl oz (250 ml) ready-made custard
ratafias

Divide the strawberries into 3 portions. Quarter one portion and mix with 2 tablespoons (30 ml) Grand Marnier. Whip the cream and vanilla essence until starting to thicken. Dissolve the gelatine in 4 tablespoons (60 ml) of warm water and mix with the cream and custard. Stir in the strawberries in Grand Marnier. Spoon into a 2 pint (1 litre) soufflé dish. Chill for 3–4 hours. Purée the second portion of the strawberries with the remaining Grand Marnier. Spread the last portion of strawberries on top of the cream and cover with some of the purée. Decorate the sides of the cream by pressing ratafia biscuits on to the sides. Serve with the remaining purée.

Lemon soufflé
Serves 8 (or 20 as part of a buffet)

We seem to be quite partial to lemon desserts in our family, perhaps because we like quite rich dishes and like to freshen our palates after a rich main course.

2 eggs, separated
6 oz (150 g) caster sugar
grated rind and juice of 3 lemons
1 sachet gelatine (½ oz/12 g)
10 fl oz (250 ml) double cream, whipped lightly
flaked hazelnuts to decorate

Beat the egg-yolks with the caster sugar and lemon juice. Stir in the rind and dissolve the gelatine as instructed on the packet. Whip the egg-whites until stiff. Stir in the gelatine, cream and egg-whites. Spoon into a serving bowl and leave to set. Decorate with hazelnuts just before serving.

6 Sunday Lunch

I am an avid fan of Sunday lunch. Our family live too far away to get together often, and when we do, if it is not to celebrate a special occasion it will probably be for a traditional Sunday lunch. One thing that has changed over the years, however, has been the move towards a lighter meal in the summer months – it seems a shame to waste a glorious summer afternoon just because you have eaten too much! During the winter months, however, we are perfectly happy to sit down to a roast meal with all the trimmings – and this is one time when we always opt for a traditional pudding!

Suggested menus
(Recipes are given in the order shown below)

Winter roast
Roast rib of beef
Horseradish cream
Gravy
Roast potatoes
Yorkshire pudding
Baked cauliflower gratin
Carrots and peas

Tarte tartin

Drinks
Red wine

Summer Sunday lunch
Salmon en croûte
New potatoes and summer vegetables
or
Selection of salads
Mayonnaise

Summer pudding

Drinks
White wine

Other suggested recipes
Roast pork
Orange roasted lamb
Cider roasted lamb
Boned stuffed chicken
Cashew, parsnip and mushroom roast
Roast swedes
Roasted vegetable platter
Pumpkin and sweet potato mash
Oven baked rösti
New potatoes, Mediterranean style
Apple sauce
Madeira and mushroom sauce
Apple crumble
Rhubarb crisp
Brioche and butter pudding
Hot choc 'n' nut cheesecake
Treacle tart
Lemon tart
Charlotte russe

Roast rib of beef
Serves 6–8

There is no doubt that the favourite British dish for Sunday lunch is roast beef, and it is certainly the roast that I would serve to a foreign visitor. It has also to be admitted that it is a very expensive treat nowadays. Still, for a special family Sunday gathering I think it is money well spent, and I would still rather have a good rib of beef only occasionally than substitute a cheaper cut of beef. Traditionally we always have this joint either on Boxing Day or the following day – and it is always cooked by the menfolk! (After all, if the girls have been responsible for the Christmas turkey it is only fair to let the boys take their turn – and it is wonderful to return from the pub to that beautiful aroma wafting through the house!)

> 6 lb (2.4 kg) rib joint of beef
> sprinkling of mustard powder
> sprinkling of plain flour
> salt and pepper
> a few onion slices
> knob of beef dripping

Pre-heat the oven to 230°C/450°F/Gas 8. Heat the beef dripping in a roasting tin while sprinkling the fat surfaces of the beef with the mustard and flour. Season well. When the beef dripping is hot add the beef and onion slices to the tin. Roast in the pre-heated oven for 20 minutes. Baste the meat and turn the heat down to 190°C/375°F/Gas 5. Continue to cook the beef for 1¾ hours for medium rare beef and 2¼ hours for well-done meat. Baste frequently during cooking. Leave in a warm place, covered in foil, for at least 20 minutes before carving.

 NB: If you want to use a boneless rolled rib of beef, you will need a 4 lb (1.6 kg) joint. After the initial cooking, turn the temperature down to 180°C/350°F/Gas 4 and cook for 1½ hours for medium rare and 2¼ hours for well-done meat.

Horseradish cream
Serves 6–8

> 5 fl oz (125 ml) double cream
> 2 tablespoons (30 ml) fresh grated horseradish
> 1 tablespoon (15 ml) lemon juice
> 1 tablespoon (15 ml) wholegrain mustard

Lightly whip the cream and then stir in the other ingredients.

Gravy
Serves 6–8

I have an aversion to making gravy. I think it is because my mother makes such good gravy that I have never really felt happy with my efforts – and because some of my earliest attempts were dismal lumpy flops! Still, I can now make a passable effort, but I still sometimes resort to packeted mixes – or pass the job to someone else! (It must be the coward in me – gravy holds no horrors for Andy!)

1 tablespoon (15 ml) plain flour
2 tablespoons (30 ml) fat from roasting tin
1 pint (500 ml) vegetable stock
5 fl oz (125 ml) red wine
5 fl oz (125 ml) dry Madeira or sherry
salt and pepper

Add the flour to the roasting tin in which you have the fat, and, over a low heat, mix the fat and flour to a paste. Gradually whisk in the stock and when this is bubbling add the wine and Madeira. Season to taste.

Roast potatoes
Serves 6–8

Because my mother has always produced such excellent roast potatoes I never really felt happy with my efforts. But in this area I am happy to say that I am now totally confident in myself. This is my recipe for perfect roast potatoes.

> 3 lb (1.2 kg) potatoes, cut into chunks
> sprinkling of paprika
> salt and pepper
> 3 oz (75 g) beef dripping

Pre-heat the oven to 220°C/425°F/Gas 7. Par-boil the potatoes. Drain. I usually rough the edges up a little with a fork (this makes them crispier on the outside). Sprinkle with paprika, salt and pepper. Meanwhile, melt the beef dripping until very hot and then tip the potatoes in, stirring them so that they are covered in fat. Cook in the pre-heated oven for 40 minutes until brown and crisp.

Yorkshire pudding
Serves 6–8

With the Yorkshire pudding it was my gran whom everyone envied! However, I have found that this recipe gives excellent results. I like to make the Yorkshire with a mixture of milk and water. Try it both ways to see which you prefer.

>   2 eggs
>   6 oz (150 g) plain flour
>   10 fl oz (250 ml) milk, or 6 fl oz (150 ml) milk plus 4 fl oz (100 ml) water
>   salt
>   2–3 tablespoons (30–45 ml) beef dripping, melted

Pre-heat the oven to 220°C/425°F/Gas 7. Whisk the eggs into the flour and then whisk in the milk or milk and water mixture. Season with a good pinch of salt. Meanwhile, heat the beef dripping in a roasting tin in the oven. When hot, pour the batter in and bake in the pre-heated oven for 35–40 minutes until well risen, brown and crisp. Serve immediately.

For really good Yorkshire puddings it is essential that you get the beef dripping really hot before adding the batter – and that the oven is nice and hot. Yorkshire puddings also make a good choice for weekday meals, served with sausages and onion gravy – absolutely yummy!

Baked cauliflower gratin
Serves 6–8

 1½–2 lb (600–800 g) cauliflower, in florets
 1 oz (25 g) butter
 1 oz (25 g) flour
 10 fl oz (250 ml) milk
 4 tablespoons (60 ml) single cream
 3 oz (75 g) Cheddar cheese, grated
 3 oz (75 g) fresh breadcrumbs
 salt and pepper

Pre-heat the oven to 200°C/400°F/Gas 6. Boil, microwave or steam the cauliflower until it is cooked but still has some 'bite'. Meanwhile make a white sauce: heat the butter, stir in the flour with a little milk, and continue gradually adding the milk until all is incorporated. Cook the sauce for 2 minutes. Combine with the cream and season. Lay the cauliflower in a gratin dish and cover with the sauce. Mix the breadcrumbs and cheese together and sprinkle over the sauce. Cook in the pre-heated oven for 30–40 minutes.

Tarte Tatin
Serves 6–8

This is an extremely rich dish with lots of lovely caramel sauce – yummy!

 2 lb (800 g) dessert apples, cored and peeled
 4 oz (100 g) butter
 4 oz (100 g) soft dark brown sugar
 8 oz (200 g) puff pastry

Pre-heat the oven to 220°C/425°F/Gas 7. Cut each apple into thick rings. Place the butter, sugar and apples into an ovenproof and flameproof 8 inch (20 cm) dish. Heat on the hob until the butter and sugar caramelize. Roll out the puff pastry to cover the apples, tucking the edges of the pastry tightly into the dish. Bake in the pre-heated oven for 15–20 minutes, until brown and well risen. Serve immediately, with vanilla ice-cream or cream.

Salmon en croûte
Serves 6–8

This makes an excellent summer dinner party dish and it is a particular favourite for Sunday lunch – served hot with new potatoes and vegetables or cold with assorted salads. It really is extremely easy to make. Once you have done it a few times you may feel confident about using a smaller amount of pastry than I have suggested here – but for novices at this dish I feel that it is safer to start with a reasonable amount of pastry as it makes it so much easier to handle. For those feeling artistic can I suggest making fins and tails out of pastry and adding these in the appropriate places – the final appearance is completely up to you.

1½ lb (600 g) puff pastry
2 lb (800 g) salmon tail fillets, skinned
4 oz (100 g) cod fillet, skinned
4 oz (100 g) cooked, peeled prawns
4 oz (100 g) smoked salmon
1 tablespoon (15 ml) chopped fresh parsley
1 tablespoon (15 ml) chopped fresh chives
grated rind and juice of 1 lemon
1 egg, beaten
2 tablespoons (30 ml) melted butter
salt and pepper
egg to glaze

Pre-heat the oven to 200°C/400°F/Gas 6. Roll out half the pastry to an oval about 1 inch (2.5 cm) bigger than your salmon fillets. Place the pastry on a non-stick baking tin and place one fillet in the middle of the pastry. Blend together the cod, prawns, smoked salmon, herbs, lemon, beaten egg, and butter. Season well. Spread over salmon and top with the other fillet. Roll out the rest of the pastry to cover fish completely. Press the edges together to seal. Use the tip of a spoon to mark scales all over the pastry. Glaze with beaten egg and bake in the pre-heated oven for about 40 minutes, until the pastry is crisp and brown.

New potatoes
Serves 6–8

> 2 lb (800 g) new potatoes
> sprig of mint (optional)
> melted butter
> chopped fresh herbs – mint or parsley
> salt

Do not peel the potatoes – if they are the loose-skinned type, scrape them. Any larger specimens should be cut in half. Bring a saucepan of water to the boil and *then* add the potatoes. Add the mint if using. Reduce the heat a little and cook at a soft rolling boil for about 12 minutes (but some may take up to 20 minutes). Drain, and serve coated in melted butter and chopped herbs (or some people prefer them plain but with a good sprinkling of salt).

Summer vegetables
Serves 6–8

We are extremely lucky in that we live in a region which has many p-y-o farms, and in the summer we like to get out on a Sunday morning and pick the vegetables for Sunday lunch. The freshness of the vegetables really shines through in this dish.

> 8 oz (200 g) baby carrots
> 8 oz (200 g) broad beans
> 8 oz (200 g) mangetout
> 8 oz (200 g) baby courgettes
> 1 oz (25 g) butter
> grated rind and juice of 1 lemon
> 1 tablespoon (15 ml) chopped chives
> 1 tablespoon (15 ml) chopped mint or tarragon

Boil, steam or microwave the vegetables until tender. Melt the butter and add to the lemon and herbs. Use to coat the vegetables before serving.

Potato salad
Serves 6–8

1½ lb (600 g) salad potatoes
5 fl oz (125 ml) mayonnaise
3 tablespoons (45 ml) salad cream
2 tablespoons (30 ml) olive oil
1 tablespoon (15 ml) white wine vinegar
1 tablespoon (15 ml) lemon juice
sprinkling of chives
salt and pepper

Boil, steam or microwave the potatoes until tender. Drain, cool and then slice. Mix the rest of the ingredients together and use to coat the potatoes.

Summer pudding
Serves 6–8

12 oz (300 g) white bread, 2–3 days old
2 lb (800 g) mixed summer fruits
4 oz (100 g) caster sugar
4 tablespoons (60 ml) water

Cut the crusts off the bread and use to line a 2 pint (1 litre) pudding basin. Reserve some of the bread to cover the top. Heat the fruit, sugar and water together until the sugar dissolves and the fruit juices flow. Spoon the fruit into the basin with half the juices. Cover with the reserved bread and spoon more juice over this. Place a saucer over the base and weight it down. Refrigerate overnight. To serve, invert on to a serving plate and pour the remaining juices over and around the pudding.

Roast pork
Serves 6–8

> 4 lb (1.6 kg) boned and rolled joint of pork
> a few slices of onion
> sprinkling of thyme
> salt and pepper

Pre-heat the oven to 220°C/425°F/Gas 7. Place the pork joint in a roasting tin with the onion underneath, sprinkle with the thyme and season with salt and pepper. Cook in the pre-heated oven for 30 minutes. Reduce the heat to 190°C/375°F/Gas 5 and cook for a further 1¾–2 hours. Leave the meat in a warm place for 20 minutes before carving. Remove the crackling and serve separately.

Orange roasted lamb
Serves 4–6

This is a popular roast with whoever is cooking, as it virtually takes care of itself and doesn't take very long to cook. The only snag is remembering actually to put the meat into the marinade – and of course finding a butcher who will bone the meat for you. When you ask for it to be boned, you will usually find they scowl at you – however, once you have explained that you are not stuffing it and it doesn't need to be rolled, the smiles will return.

> 2–3 lb (800 g–1.2 kg) leg of lamb, boned
> 10 fl oz (250 ml) orange juice
> 1 tablespoon (15 ml) runny honey
> 1 tablespoon (15 ml) soy sauce
> 1 tablespoon (15 ml) cider vinegar
> 2 cloves garlic, sliced
> 1 sprig rosemary
> 1 teaspoon (5 ml) ginger purée

Marinade the lamb in the other ingredients overnight or for a minimum of 8 hours. Pre-heat the oven to 200°C/400°F/Gas 6. Open up the lamb and lay it flat on a roasting rack in a tray. (The meat that was next to the bone should be facing down). Pour the marinade mixture over the lamb and cook in the pre-heated oven for 20 minutes. Baste the lamb and turn the heat down to 180°C/350°F/Gas 4. Cook for another 30–45 minutes. While carving the meat, keep the marinade warm, to serve as a gravy. If the gravy is too fatty for your taste, skim off some of the fat, add a little orange juice or red wine, and thicken with a little cornflower or arrowroot.

Cider roasted lamb
Serves 6–8

    1 leg of lamb
    1 pint (500 ml) sparkling dry cider
    sprig of rosemary, chopped
    salt and pepper

Pre-heat the oven to 180°C/350°F/Gas 4. Place the lamb on a rack in a roasting tin. Pour the cider over the meat and season with the rosemary, salt and pepper. Roast in the pre-heated oven for 30 minutes per lb/500 g. Baste occasionally with the cider. Rest for 20 minutes before carving. When making your gravy use the cider in the bottom of the pan instead of the red wine and half of the stock.

Boned stuffed chicken
Serves 6–8

I did once bone my own chicken – it's not particularly difficult, but it is time-consuming. I now ask my butcher to do it – after all, he's the expert and why should I do something that will take me ages when he can do it in minutes? Just don't ask for this service on a busy Saturday morning with a long queue behind you!

12 oz (300 g) stoned prunes, soaked overnight in
  orange juice
8 oz (200 g) cooked brown rice
bunch of spring onions, chopped
2 cloves garlic, crushed
2 tablespoons (30 ml) double cream
1 tablespoon (15 ml) chopped fresh parsley
2 tablespoons (30 ml) medium sherry
a 3.5–4 lb (1.4–1.6 kg) chicken, boned
salt and pepper
softened butter

Pre-heat the oven to 190°C/375°F/Gas 5. Chop up the prunes and combine with the rice, spring onions, garlic, cream, parsley and sherry. Season. Use to stuff the chicken. Fold the chicken over the stuffing and sew up with string. Cover with softened butter and roast in the pre-heated oven for 1¼ hours, or until the chicken is cooked through and brown. Cover in foil and leave to cool. Slice thinly to serve.

Cashew, parsnip and mushroom roast
Serves 6–8

This makes a good vegetarian alternative for a Sunday
lunch, served with Madeira and mushroom sauce (page
116) or onion sauce (page 206).

1 onion, chopped
2 cloves garlic, crushed
1 tablespoon (15 ml) olive oil
8 oz (200 g) cashew nuts
4 oz (100 g) fresh breadcrumbs
1 egg, beaten
1 lb (400 g) parsnips, cooked and mashed
1 tablespoon (15 ml) chopped fresh chives
1 tablespoon (15 ml) chopped fresh thyme
5 fl oz (125 ml) vegetable stock
salt and pepper
8 oz (200 g) mushrooms, sliced
knob of butter

Pre-heat the oven to 180°C/350°F/Gas 4. Fry the onion and
garlic in the oil until soft. Blend with all the other
ingredients except the mushrooms and butter. Season
well. Cook the mushrooms in the butter until soft. Into a
greased 2 lb (800 g) loaf tin put a few mushrooms. Cover
with half the nut mixture. Layer the rest of mushrooms in
the tin and cover with the rest of the nut mixture. Cover
with foil and cook in the pre-heated oven for 1 hour.
Leave in the tin for 10 minutes before turning out. Serve
hot or cold.

Roast swedes
Serves 4–6

2 lb (800 g) swede, cut into large chunks
olive oil
salt and pepper

Pre-heat the oven to 200°C/400°F/Gas 6. Heat the oil in a roasting tin and add the swede. Mix thoroughly, so that the swede is coated in oil. Season well. Bake in the pre-heated oven for 1-1¼ hours. Turn occasionally and baste.

Roasted vegetable platter
Serves 4–6

Don't be put off by the garlic in this recipe (unless you're related to vampires) – when garlic cloves are roasted they have a milder, creamier taste. If you manage to get hold of some elephant garlic it is ideal for this dish – but you can cut down on the number of cloves used as they are so much larger than normal cloves.

2 parsnips, quartered
2 carrots, quartered
1 swede, cut into chunks
2 small red onions, quartered
3 tablespoons (45 ml) olive oil
sprinkling of rosemary
8–12 cloves garlic (unpeeled)
salt and pepper

Pre-heat the oven to 200°C/400°F/Gas 6. Put all the vegetables into a large roasting tin and pour in the olive oil. Mix well. Add the herbs, garlic and seasoning. Cover with foil and bake in the pre-heated oven for 40 minutes. Remove the cover and turn the vegetables, then return the tin to the oven for 20 minutes or until the vegetables are brown.

Pumpkin and sweet potato mash
Serves 6–8

I am including this recipe for my cousin Siân, who was
very keen on it when she had it at our house and who
swears that the recipe I gave her over the phone didn't
taste the same. I am sure that this is the version that we
had that day! (Honest.)

> 1½ lb (600 g) pumpkin, seeded and diced
> 12 oz (300 g) sweet potato, diced
> 3 oz (75 g) butter
> 1 tablespoon (15 ml) soft dark brown sugar
> salt and pepper
> pinch of ground ginger

Boil or microwave the pumpkin and sweet potato until
tender. Strain and then mash. Melt the butter in a
saucepan and add the mashed pumpkin and potato. Mix
in the sugar and cook until the butter has absorbed.
Season well and add ginger to taste. Can be kept,
covered, in a warm oven for 30 minutes.

Oven baked rösti
Serves 6–8

> 2 lb (800 g) potatoes
> salt and pepper
> 2 oz (50 g) butter

Pre-heat the oven to 200°C/400°F/Gas 6. Par-boil the potatoes, cool, and then grate coarsely. Season well. Melt half
the butter in a large ovenproof dish. Press the potatoes
down firmly into the dish and dot with the remaining
butter. Cook in the pre-heated oven for 50–60 minutes,
until brown.

New potatoes, Mediterranean style
Serves 4–6

> 1½–2 lb (600–800 g) small new potatoes, cleaned
> 10 fl oz (250 ml) olive oil
> 5 fl oz (125 ml) red wine
> chopped fresh parsley to garnish
> salt and pepper

Gently hit the potatoes with a rolling pin, just enough to cause cracks to appear (not so that they are flattened or break in half – husbands please note!). In a large frying pan, heat the oil till it is very hot and fry a few potatoes at a time, to brown on all sides, removing them as they brown. Pour off the oil and return all the potatoes to the pan with the wine. Cover and bring to the boil, then turn the heat down and simmer gently for 10–15 minutes (or until potatoes are cooked). Garnish with parsley and season. These will keep warm for a while in a warm oven. However, they can also be served cold, and for this I suggest adding 2 tablespoons (30 ml) olive oil whilst still hot, and then leaving to cool. I also sometimes add a little tomato purée and red pesto, depending on what I am serving them with.

Apple sauce
Serves 6–8

1 lb (400 g) Bramley apples, peeled, cored and
  sliced
2 tablespoons (30 ml) water
knob of butter
sugar to taste

Put the apples, water and butter into a small saucepan.
Cover and cook until the apple has 'pulped'. Purée and
sugar to taste. Serve hot or cold.

Madeira and mushroom sauce
Serves 6-8

8 oz (200 g) mushrooms, finely chopped
2 oz (50 g) butter
5 fl oz (125 ml) Madeira (dry)
1 tablespoon (15 ml) plain flour
15 fl oz (375 ml) vegetable stock
salt and pepper

Cook the mushrooms in the butter until soft. Add the
Madeira and simmer for a few minutes. Stir in the flour
and then gradually add the stock. Simmer for 5 minutes.
Season to taste and serve.

Apple crumble
Serves 4–8

    2 lb (800 g) Bramley apples, cut into chunks
    2 tablespoons (30 ml) butter
    2 tablespoons (30 ml) caster sugar
    3 oz (75 g) self-raising wholemeal flour
    3 oz (75 g) soft dark brown sugar
    3 oz (75 g) butter, chopped

Pre-heat the oven to 200°C/400°F/Gas 6. Cook the apples with the 2 tablespoons of butter, until soft but not falling apart. Mix the apples and 2 tablespoons of caster sugar together and place in a pie dish. Mix together the flour, soft dark brown sugar and chopped butter. Rub the mixture between your fingertips until it resembles bread-crumbs. Cover the fruit with the crumb mixture. Bake in the pre-heated oven for 30 minutes until brown. Serve with vanilla ice-cream, custard or cream.

A number of other fruit crumbles can be made, and here are some good mixes.

APPLE AND RHUBARB CRUMBLE
Replace 1 lb (400 g) of apples with 1 lb (400 g) of rhubarb. Cut into chunks – do not pre-cook. Just add with the caster sugar.

APPLE AND BLACKBERRY CRUMBLE
Replace 1 lb (400 g) of the apples with 12 oz (300 g) of blackberries. Do not pre-cook, and add with the caster sugar.

APPLE AND APRICOT CRUMBLE
Replace 1 lb (400 g) of the apples with 1 lb (400 g) of fresh apricots. Remove the stones and cut into quarters. Do not pre-cook, and add with the caster sugar.

Rhubarb crisp
Serves 4–6

>2 lb (800 g) rhubarb, sliced
>2 tablespoons (30 ml) butter
>honey or sugar to taste
>6 oz (150 g) fresh wholemeal breadcrumbs
>2 oz (50 g) soft dark brown sugar
>2 oz (50 g) butter

Cook the rhubarb with the 2 tablespoons of butter until soft. Blend to a purée and sweeten to taste with honey or sugar. Cool. Meanwhile, fry the breadcrumbs and sugar in butter until brown and starting to crisp. Cool. When both are cool, layer the rhubarb purée and breadcrumbs into a serving bowl, finishing with a layer of breadcrumbs. Serve with cream.

APPLE CRISP
This can be made by substituting the rhubarb with 2 lb (800 g) Bramley apples, diced.

APPLE AND RASPBERRY OR BLACKBERRY CRISP
For the 2 lb (800 g) rhubarb substitute 1 lb (400 g) of Bramley apples, diced, and 12 oz (300 g) of fresh raspberries or blackberries.

Brioche and butter pudding
Serves 4–8

This recipe is adapted from the humble bread and butter pudding, of course. We tried it once and were totally converted. It is absolutely delicious.

> 1 brioche loaf or 4 brioche rolls
> butter
> sprinkling of raisins and sultanas
> 1 pint (500 ml) milk
> 4 eggs, beaten

Pre-heat the oven to 180°C/350°F/Gas 4. Cut the loaf or rolls into 16 slices. Butter each and place half the slices into an ovenproof dish. Sprinkle with the dried fruit and top with the rest of the brioche slices (butter side up). Beat together the milk and eggs and pour over the brioche slices. Push the slices down into the milk and egg mixture. Bake in the pre-heated oven for 30–40 minutes, until brown and well-risen.

Hot choc 'n' nut cheesecake
Serves 6–8

8 oz (200 g) chocolate digestive biscuits, crushed
4 oz (100 g) butter, melted
2 eggs, separated
3 oz (75 g) soft dark brown sugar
8 oz (200 g) curd cheese
5 fl oz (125 ml) double cream
2 oz (50 g) pecan nuts, finely chopped
1 oz (25 g) cocoa powder, sifted
icing or vanilla sugar to serve

Pre-heat the oven to 170°C/325°F/Gas 3. Mix together the biscuit crumbs and butter and use to line an 8 inch (20 cm) loose-bottomed cake tin. Cover the bottom of the tin and press the crumbs around the base of the sides. Whisk the egg-yolks and brown sugar until thick and creamy, then whisk in the curd cheese, cream, nuts and cocoa powder. Whisk the egg-whites until very stiff and gently fold into the cheesecake mixture. Pour into the biscuit base and bake in the pre-heated oven for 1½ hours or until risen. Sprinkle with icing or vanilla sugar and serve hot.

Treacle tart
Serves 6–8

In the depths of winter I think this is one of the most popular puddings that you can offer. I know it always goes very quickly whenever it is on offer at my house.

1 lb (400 g) shortcrust pastry
1 egg, beaten
5 tablespoons (75 ml) golden syrup
1 tablespoon (15 ml) black treacle
2 oz (50 g) ground almonds
3 oz (75 g) fresh white breadcrumbs
1 lemon, grated rind and 1 tablespoon (15 ml) juice
3 tablespoons (45 ml) double cream, and extra to serve

Pre-heat the oven to 190°C/375°F/Gas 5. Use three-quarters of the pastry to roll out and fit an 8 inch (20 cm) flan tin. Reserve a little of the egg and beat the rest of the ingredients together. Pour into the pastry case. Roll out the remaining pastry and cut into strips. Twist each strip a little and use these to make a lattice cover for the top of the tart. Glaze with the reserved egg and bake in the pre-heated oven for 25–30 minutes until golden brown. Serve with cream.

Lemon tart
Serves 4–6

12 oz (300 g) shortcrust pastry
4 eggs, beaten
2 oz (50 g) caster sugar
juice and rind of 2 large lemons
5 fl oz (125 ml) double cream

Pre-heat the oven to 200°C/400°F/Gas 6. Line a 9 inch (22.5 cm) round tin with the pastry and bake 'blind' for 20 minutes. Beat together the eggs and caster sugar until light and creamy. Stir in the other ingredients and use to fill the pastry case. Reduce the heat to 180°C/350°F/Gas 4 and cook for 25–35 minutes, until the tart is set.

Charlotte russe
Serves 4–6

Patience is a virtue when it comes to turning out a charlotte russe. You are supposed to help it out by standing the tin in warm water, briefly. I usually can't be bothered with this and find that if I dig around the sides with a knife and give it a good tap, it will come out. This method is not foolproof, however, so I only make a charlotte russe for immediate family or close friends – then I don't feel too worried about turning it out (and usually if you're not worried it comes out easily!). My mother-in-law is an expert in these – and I have never made one for her! (It's the coward in me coming out again.)

> 1 sachet raspberry jelly crystals made up to 15 fl oz (375 ml)
> 8 oz (200 g) mixed raspberries and redcurrants
> 5 fl oz (125 ml) double cream
> 5 fl oz (125 ml) ready-made custard
> 15–16 sponge fingers
> 1 sachet gelatine (½ oz/12 g)

Using raspberry crystals (enough to make 1 pint/500 ml), make up 15 fl oz (375 ml) raspberry jelly. Pour a little into the bottom of a 2 pint (1 litre) charlotte mould. Put into the refrigerator. After 15–20 minutes it will have set. Arrange some of the redcurrants and raspberries on the jelly. Cover with more of the liquid jelly (you will now have used about 5 fl oz/125 ml), and return the dish to the refrigerator for 15–20 minutes. Whip the cream until starting to thicken. Add the custard and the rest of the jelly and fruit. When the jelly in the mould is starting to set, arrange the sponge fingers around the edge of the mould (you will have to cut off part of the fingers to fit them in). Dissolve the gelatine in 3 tablespoons (45 ml) of hot water and mix with the cream mixture. Now pour the cream mixture into the mould. Cover with clingfilm and leave to set overnight.

7 Time for Tea

When families live within a reasonable distance of each other, teatime provides a popular excuse just to 'pop in'. It certainly provides grandparents with an ideal way of seeing their grandchildren without anyone feeling imposed upon.

In many families, too, it is not always possible to eat together as a family in the evening, and tea becomes an important meal for small children. Sandwiches are very nutritious, and small children also need a shot of carbohydrate by late afternoon, as their energy needs are much higher than ours.

There are also many other occasions when a home-baked cake comes in useful – for birthdays or as a treat for visitors. Certainly if you are married to a fanatical cricketer, as I am, at some point you will be called upon to provide a cricket tea!

Tea is a meal that I am becoming increasingly fond of. There is very little work involved and it is a pleasant interlude in a busy day, when people can gather together and just gossip a little. I would heartily recommend its encouragement.

Suggested menu
(Recipes are given in the order shown below)

Choice of 2 or 3 types of sandwich
Lamingtons
Orange gingerbread
Cherry and almond loaf
Seed cake

Other suggested recipes
Rock cakes
Chocolate brownies
Madeleines
Orange syrup cake
Lemon cake
Coconut cake
Raspberry sponge
Apple cake
Northumbrian sweet pastries
Fruit 'n' nut tarts

Sandwiches

These are useful items when catering for a variety of occasions. There are an infinite number of fillings, and by varying the bread used you can always come up with something new. Just one word of warning – they always seem to take longer to make than you think they will! So do give yourself plenty of time.

QUANTITIES

These are difficult to give exactly, as people will use different amounts when spreading the butter or margarine and some will be more or less generous with fillings. Generally, I just keep going until I run out of one ingredient and then continue with the next. An average large loaf will contain about 22 slices. This makes 11 rounds (a round being 2 slices plus filling). It is then up to you, depending on who you are catering for, to decide whether to cut each round into 2, 3 or 4 triangles (the usual way of serving sandwiches). For hale and hearty eaters (e.g. the cricket club) you would usually cut each round into 2 sandwiches, while for a more delicate affair you would probably choose to cut the round into 4. It is usual to allow 1–1½ rounds per person, but for large numbers, when other items are on offer, reduce this to ¾ round per person.

Chicken sandwiches

1 wholemeal loaf
6–8 oz (150–200 g) soft margarine or butter
1 chicken, cooked and cooled, with meat removed
   from bone
10 fl oz (250 ml) mayonnaise
salt and pepper
watercress to garnish

Lay out all the slices from the loaf (in matching pairs). Spread with the margarine or butter. Mix together the chicken and mayonnaise. Season. Now spread the mixture over half the slices of bread (1 for each matching pair). Spread the mixture right up to the edges of the bread. Garnish with watercress (but leave some sandwiches without – there is always someone who doesn't like any garnish at all). Cover with the other bread slices. Cut each round into your chosen number of sandwiches. Put on to serving platters and cover with clingfilm or pack into plastic boxes until needed.

CURRIED CHICKEN SANDWICHES
These are a very popular alternative to plain chicken sandwiches. Add some medium curry paste mixed with cream and some mango chutney to the chicken and mayonnaise mixture.

CHICKEN AND TARRAGON MUSTARD SANDWICHES
Add a little tarragon mustard to the chicken and mayonnaise mixture.

Ham sandwiches

1 white loaf
6–8 oz (150–200 g) soft margarine or butter
1 lb (400 g) good ham from the deli
English mustard

Again, lay out all the bread slices first in matching pairs. Spread with margarine or butter. On half the bread slices lay out the ham, and spread the other half thinly with mustard. (Again, leave a few without mustard for those who like their food plain.) Cover the ham with its matching bread slice and cut each round into the required number of sandwiches. Cover or pack until required.

Ham, cream cheese and cress sandwiches

The ham sandwiches above are rather robust. For a more delicate affair, blend ham, cream cheese, softened margarine and cress together. These spread easily and are less likely to fall apart when being handled and eaten, so are more popular when decorum is important!

Cheese sandwiches

1 wholemeal loaf
6–8 oz (150–200 g) soft margarine or butter
1 lb (400 g) mature Cheddar cheese, grated
8 oz (200 g) soft cheese spread
salt and pepper

Lay out the bread slices and spread with margarine or butter. Mix together the cheeses and season well. Use to spread over half of the bread slices. Top with the rest of the bread and cut and keep as required.

There are many variations on the plain cheese sandwich:

CHEESE AND PICKLE
Add your chosen pickle to the cheeses when you mix them together.

CHEESE AND ONION
Add grated onion to the cheese mix.

CHEESE AND TOMATO
Once you have spread the cheeses on the bread, top with slices of tomato before covering with the rest of the bread.

CHEESE AND CUCUMBER
The same as the cheese and tomato, substituting cucumber slices for the tomato.

CHEESE AND CELERY
Add chopped celery to the cheese mix before spreading.

Cucumber sandwiches

1 white loaf
10 oz (250 g) cream cheese
3–4 oz (75–100g) soft margarine or butter
1–2 cucumbers, sliced thinly
salt and pepper

Lay out the bread slices. Mix together the cream cheese and margarine and spread over the bread slices. Now lay out the cucumber slices over half of the bread. Season well and top with the remaining bread. Cut and keep as required.

Egg mayonnaise sandwiches

I have a phobia about egg mayonnaise sandwiches. When I was sixteen I worked one summer holiday in a factory. During a break I bought a roll which I thought contained cheese (which I adore), but unfortunately when I bit into it I found it contained egg mayonnaise. I was promptly sick! I have no idea why I dislike them so much but I can't stomach them at all. So since they are an essential part of cricket teas, this is always a job for Andy.

> 1 white loaf
> 6–8 oz (150–200 g) soft margarine or butter
> 12 hard-boiled eggs, shelled and chopped
> 10 fl oz (250 ml) mayonnaise
> 1 punnet of mustard and cress
> salt and pepper

Lay out the bread slices and spread with the margarine or butter. Mix the eggs and mayonnaise together, season well, and use this mixture to spread over half the bread slices. Sprinkle with the mustard and cress (leaving a few plain). Cover with the remaining bread slices. Cut and keep as required.

CURRIED EGG SANDWICHES
To the egg mayonnaise mixture add some medium curry paste mixed with cream. We usually substitute watercress for the mustard and cress when making these.

EGG AND SARDINE SANDWICHES
Substitute 12 oz (300 g) canned sardines in tomato sauce for 6 of the hard-boiled eggs.

Tuna sandwiches

   1 wholemeal loaf
   6–8 oz (150–200 g) soft margarine or butter
   24 oz (600 g) canned tuna in brine, drained
   10 fl oz (250 ml) mayonnaise
   salt and pepper

Lay out the bread slices and spread with the margarine or butter. Mix the tuna and mayonnaise together and season well. Use this mixture to spread over half the bread. Top with the remaining slices. Cut and keep as required.

TUNA AND ONION SANDWICHES
Add some grated onion to the tuna and mayonnaise mixture.

TUNA AND PICKLE
Add your chosen pickle to the tuna and mayonnaise mixture.

TUNA, TOMATO AND RED PEPPER
Add some skinned chopped tomatoes and diced red pepper to the tuna and mayonnaise mixture.

TUNA AND CUCUMBER
After you have spread your bread with the tuna and mayonnaise mixture, top with thinly sliced cucumber.

Lamingtons
Makes 12

The rise of the Australian 'soap' has also given rise to the popularity of these Australian cakes. They are quick and easy to make and very 'moreish'. Don't be alarmed at what seems to be a huge amount of icing sugar in the topping. It beats down into a thick coating sauce.

3 eggs
3 oz (75 g) caster sugar
3 oz (75 g) plain flour
1 tablespoon (15 ml) cornflour
2 oz (50 g) unsalted butter, melted

To decorate
1 lb (400 g) icing sugar
3 oz (75 g) cocoa
4 fl oz (100 ml) milk
2 oz (50 g) desiccated coconut

Pre-heat the oven to 190°C/375°F/Gas 5. Beat the eggs and caster sugar together until thick and mousse-like. Stir in the flours and half the melted butter. Spoon into a greased and lined 11 × 7 inch (28 × 18 cm) baking tin. Bake in the pre-heated oven for 20–25 minutes until risen and brown. Turn on to a wire rack to cool. Cut into 12. Beat together the icing sugar, cocoa and milk and the remaining butter. Use this to cover the Lamingtons and then sprinkle with the coconut. Leave to set.

Orange gingerbread
Makes 12 portions

4 oz (100 g) golden syrup
4 oz (100 g) black treacle
4 oz (100 g) soft margarine
2 oz (50 g) soft dark brown sugar
1 teaspoon (5 ml) bicarbonate of soda
5 fl oz (125 ml) orange juice
8 oz (200 g) plain brown flour
2 teaspoons (10 ml) ground ginger
1 teaspoon (5 ml) mixed spice
2 eggs, beaten

Pre-heat the oven to 150°C/300°F/Gas 2. Melt the golden syrup, treacle, margarine and sugar. Dissolve the bicarbonate of soda in the orange juice and add. Stir well. Add the rest of the ingredients and beat well. Grease and line a 7 × 11 inch (18 × 28 cm) tin. Pour the mixture into the tin. Bake in the pre-heated oven for 1 hour. Cool in the tin, then mark into squares and serve.

Cherry and almond loaf
Makes 8–12 portions

6 oz (150 g) soft margarine
6 oz (150 g) caster sugar
4 oz (100 g) self-raising flour
3 oz (75 g) ground almonds
3 eggs, beaten
8 oz (200 g) glacé cherries, washed and halved
2 tablespoons (30 ml) milk
1 tablespoon (15 ml) preserving sugar

Pre-heat the oven to 160°C/325°F/Gas 3. Beat together the margarine, caster sugar, flour, almonds and eggs. Stir in the glacé cherries and milk. Spoon into a greased, lined 2 lb (800 g) loaf tin. Sprinkle with the preserving sugar and bake in the pre-heated oven for 50–60 minutes until risen and brown on top.

Seed cake
Makes an 8 inch (20 cm) cake

It's strange how trends come and go even in cookery – and seed cake is now becoming very popular again after many years of neglect. I think this is a lovely cake, and it also keeps very well. Do try it – it has a lovely aromatic taste.

8 oz (200 g) self-raising flour
4 oz (100 g) ground rice
8 oz (200 g) soft margarine
8 oz (200 g) caster sugar
3 eggs, beaten
5 fl oz (125 ml) milk
1 teaspoon (5 ml) vanilla essence
2 tablespoons (30 ml) caraway seeds

Pre-heat the oven to 180°C/350°F/Gas 4. Reserve 1 table-spoon (15 ml) of the caraway seeds. Beat the rest of the ingredients together. Grease and line an 8 inch (20 cm) cake tin and spoon the cake mixture into this. Sprinkle with the reserved caraway seeds and bake in the pre-heated oven for 50–60 minutes, until a skewer inserted into the middle comes out clean. Cool in the tin for 10 minutes, then turn out on to a wire rack to cool completely.

Rock cakes
Makes 8–12

8 oz (200 g) wholemeal flour
1 teaspoon (5 ml) mixed spice
4 oz (100 g) soft margarine or butter
grated rind of ½ a lemon
4 oz (100 g) demerara sugar
4 oz (100 g) mixed dried fruit
1 egg, beaten
1 tablespoon (15 ml) milk
preserving sugar for dredging

Pre-heat the oven to 200°C/400°F/Gas 6. Firstly mix together the flour, spice and margarine or butter. Stir in the rest of the ingredients. Place in small heaps on a greased baking tray and bake in the pre-heated oven for 15–20 minutes until brown. While still warm, dredge with preserving sugar.

NB: These are quite spicy – you can make them with half the amount of mixed spice.

Chocolate brownies
Makes 12 portions

6 oz (150 g) plain chocolate, melted
4 oz (100 g) soft margarine
8 oz (200 g) soft dark brown sugar
6 oz (150 g) wholemeal plain flour
4 oz (100 g) raisins
2 oz (50 g) nuts, chopped
2 eggs, beaten
1 teaspoon (5 ml) vanilla essence

Pre-heat the oven to 180°C/350°F/Gas 4. Beat all the ingredients together. Spoon into a greased, lined 7 × 11 inch (18 × 28 cm) baking tin. Bake in the pre-heated oven for 25–30 minutes. Cool in the tin, then mark into portions.

Madeleines

I have only recently started making these again – I can remember making them as a child, but to make the perfect madeleine you need a little pyramid-shaped object with a plunger that extricates the mixture. These have only recently become available again – you can now obtain them from Lakeland Plastics. They are an excellent way of keeping children busy in the kitchen on a rainy afternoon – as long as you don't mind the sticky mess that they get into!

4 oz (100 g) butter
4 oz (100 g) caster sugar
2 eggs, beaten
4 oz (100 g) self-raising flour

To decorate
glace cherries, halved
raspberry or strawberry jam
desiccated coconut

Pre-heat the oven to 180°C/350°F/Gas 4. Cream together the butter and sugar, gradually beat in the eggs and then fold in the flour. Pack the mixture into the pyramid maker and then use the plunger to press out on to a baking tray lined with non-stick baking parchment. Bake in the pre-heated oven for 20 minutes until well risen and brown. Place on a wire rack and cool. To decorate (this is the messy bit!), melt the jam and brush over the madeleines, roll in the coconut and top with half a cherry.

Orange syrup cake
Makes 8–12 portions

8 oz (200 g) soft margarine
8 oz (200 g) caster sugar
4 eggs, beaten
2 tablespoons (30 ml) ground rice
8 oz (200 g) plain flour
2 tablespoons (30 ml) baking powder
grated rind of 2 oranges
5 fl oz (125 ml) fresh orange juice
3 oz (75 g) icing sugar

Pre-heat the oven to 180°C/350°F/Gas 4. Beat together all the ingredients except the orange juice and icing sugar. Spoon the mixture into a greased, lined 2 lb (800 g) loaf tin. Bake in the pre-heated oven for 75 minutes. Heat the orange juice with the icing sugar in a small pan. Pierce the cake in several places and pour the syrup over the cake. Leave overnight to let the cake absorb the syrup. Remove from the tin and serve.

Lemon cake
Makes an 8 inch (20 cm) cake

4 oz (100 g) butter
8 oz (200 g) caster sugar
2 eggs, beaten
4 oz (100 g) self-raising flour
1 lemon, rind and juice

Pre-heat the oven to 180°C/350°F/Gas 4. Beat the butter with half the sugar until light and creamy. Beat in the eggs and then gently mix in the flour. Put in a greased, lined 8 inch (20 cm) cake tin and bake in the pre-heated oven for 40 minutes or until the cake has set and feels firm to the touch. Cool the cake for 10 minutes in the tin, then remove to a wire rack and remove the paper. Mix the remaining sugar with the lemon juice and spoon carefully over the cake. Leave to cool – a sugar crust will form on the cake.

Coconut cake
Makes an 8 inch (20 cm) cake

8 oz (200 g) self-raising flour
4 oz (100 g) ground rice
4 oz (100 g) desiccated coconut
8 oz (200 g) soft margarine
8 oz (200 g) caster sugar
3 eggs, beaten
5 fl oz (125 ml) milk

Pre-heat the oven to 170°C/325°F/Gas 3. Reserve 1 table-spoon (15 ml) of coconut for the cake topping. Beat the rest of the ingredients together. Grease and line an 8 inch (20 cm) deep cake tin and spoon the mixture into this. Sprinkle with the reserved coconut and bake in the pre-heated oven for 60–80 minutes (or until a skewer inserted into the middle of the cake comes out clean). Cool in the tin for 10 minutes before transferring to a wire rack to cool completely.

Raspberry sponge
Makes an 8 inch (20 cm) cake

When I first wrote *Grub on a Grant*, some of my friends were quite frankly amazed. One of them rang me up to congratulate me and then reminded me of an episode in a school cookery lesson when we had been making sponge cakes – and I had forgotten to add the flour to the mixture. The resulting cake was rather flat! I was also well known as always being the last to finish our practical sessions. (I have to admit I was quite good at the theory.) However, I think it was because I was so hopeless at the 'right' way of doing things that I started to develop my own methods. So for the next recipe all I'd like to say is that if you remember to add all the ingredients, it comes out beautifully.

> 5 oz (125 g) plain flour
> pinch of salt
> 4 eggs, separated
> 8 oz (200 g) caster sugar
>
> *To decorate*
> raspberry jam
> whipped cream or buttercream

Pre-heat the oven to 180°C/350°F/Gas 4. Sift the flour and salt. Beat the egg-yolks with half the sugar until very pale and creamy. Whisk the egg-whites, gradually adding the rest of the sugar, and continue whisking until the whites form stiff peaks. Very gently fold the two mixtures together. Pour into a greased and lined 8 inch (20 cm) deep cake tin. Bake in the pre-heated oven for 40–45 minutes, until well risen and brown. The cake will feel 'spongy' when pressed with the fingertips. Remove from the tin and cool on a wire rack. To decorate, split the cake into 2 or 3 layers (depending on how confident you are!). Either have a layer of cream and a layer of jam, or just split the cake in two and put the jam and cream together. Reassemble the cake and sprinkle with icing sugar.

Apple cake

Makes an 8 inch (20 cm) cake

- 8 oz (200 g) Bramley apples, peeled, cored and chopped
- 8 oz (200 g) mixed dried fruit
- 6 oz (150 g) soft dark brown sugar
- 5 fl oz (125 ml) Guinness
- 12 oz (300 g) self-raising flour
- 1 tablespoon (15 ml) mixed spice
- 6 oz (150 g) soft margarine
- 1 egg, beaten
- 1 tablespoon (15 ml) preserving sugar

Pre-heat the oven to 160°C/325°F/Gas 3. Mix the apples with the fruit, sugar and Guinness and leave to soak overnight. Put the flour, spice and margarine into a bowl and rub together with your fingertips until you have a breadcrumb-like mixture. Stir into the apple mixture with the beaten egg. Put into a greased and lined 8 inch (20 cm) deep cake tin. Sprinkle with the preserving sugar. Bake in the pre-heated oven for 1¼–1½ hours until cooked through. Cool in the tin for 10 minutes before removing to a wire rack to cool.

Northumbrian sweet pastries
Makes 8

I can remember my gran making these when I was a child. It is now more difficult to get hold of the particular tins that she used (I think that they were swiss roll tins), and if you cannot get them I suggest doubling the quantities and using an 11 × 7 inch (28 × 18 cm) tin.

1 lb (400 g) shortcrust pastry
6 oz (150 g) stoned dates, chopped
2 oz (50 g) currants
2 oz (50 g) sultanas
2 oz (50 g) walnuts, chopped
2 oz (50 g) soft dark brown sugar
2 oz (50 g) butter
4 tablespoons (60 ml) water
milk and demerara sugar to glaze

Pre-heat the oven to 190°C/375°F/Gas 5. Roll out half the pastry to cover a greased 9 × 4 inch (23 × 10 cm) tin. Put the rest of the ingredients in a pan and bring to the boil. Simmer for 10 minutes, then cool a little before spreading over the pastry. Cover with the remaining pastry and glaze with the milk and sugar. Bake in the pre-heated oven for 25–30 minutes until brown. Cool in the tin and cut into triangles to serve.

Fruit 'n' nut tarts
Makes 12

> 8 oz (200 g) rich shortcrust pastry
> 3 oz (75 g) butter
> 3 oz (75 g) soft dark brown sugar
> 8 oz (200 g) can condensed milk
> 1 oz (25 g) pecans, roughly chopped
> 1 oz (25 g) raisins

Pre-heat the oven to 220°C/425°C/Gas 7. Roll out the pastry and use to line a 12-hole bun tin. Bake blind in the pre-heated oven for 10–15 minutes until the pastry is cooked and brown. Meanwhile put the butter, sugar and milk in a small saucepan and boil for a few minutes until you have a caramel mixture. Cool for 5 minutes, then stir in the pecans and raisins. Spoon into the pastry cases and chill until set.

8 Christenings

A christening will normally take place as part of the Sunday morning service, or as a special service in the afternoon. Therefore, it may be followed by a christening lunch or tea.

If you are having a christening tea I would suggest taking recipes from the Time for Tea chapter (page 123), with the addition, of course, of a christening cake. (And if you are going to be returning from a very cold church you may want to provide a warming soup.) However, if you are going to provide lunch, you have a number of choices. Some people may wish to provide a light finger buffet – or even a formal fork buffet, which, before I actually contemplated having children, is certainly what I would have plumped for. Now, however, it is a different story. For our first child's christening we plumped for an Italian meal!

This is not as strange as it appears. Since we decided to have the christening while the babe was only a few weeks old, we thought we should have something that is easy to put together and that required very little effort on the actual day when we returned from church. Since we were inviting friends who had small children of their own, we also wanted something that was informal – and in my mind, Italians and children are inextricably linked. Therefore, we came up with the idea of an Italian meal that, if the weather was good, would be set up in the garden – otherwise the house would have to just bulge a little! All the preparation was done beforehand. The only hot dishes to be served were for the main course, and these were put in the oven when we returned from church to be ready after we had enjoyed some dips and crudités. Nothing could be easier.

Suggested menus
(Recipes are given in the order shown below)

Christening tea
See Time for Tea chapter.

Italian meal
Dips and crudités (see pages 34-6)

Roast chicken, Italian style
Broccoli, mushroom and walnut gratin
Fennel gratin
Selection of salads

Tiramisu or ice-cream
Christening cake (see page 187)

Drinks
Red and white wine
Soft drinks
Champagne with the cake

Roast chicken, Italian style
Serves 10 (or 20 as part of a buffet)

2 × 3.5 lb (1.4 kg) corn-fed chickens
2 lb (800 g) new potatoes, quartered
2 onions, sliced
4 sprigs of fresh rosemary
40 cloves garlic, unpeeled
10 fl oz (250 ml) olive oil

You will need 2 large roasting tins for this dish. Pre-heat the oven to 220°C/425°F/Gas 7. Cut each chicken into pieces – 2 wings, 2 legs and 6 pieces of breast. Discard the carcass. Place all the ingredients into the roasting tins and roast in the pre-heated oven for 20 minutes. Stir all the ingredients. Turn the heat down to 190°C/375°F/Gas 5 and continue cooking for a further 20–40 minutes until the chicken is cooked and the potatoes are crisp. Serve hot.

Broccoli, mushroom and walnut gratin
Serves 10 (or 20 as part of a buffet)

3 lb (1.2 kg) broccoli
1 lb (400 g) mushrooms, quartered
4 cloves garlic, crushed
olive oil
15 fl oz (375 ml) cheese sauce
4 oz (100 g) fresh wholemeal breadcrumbs
4 oz (100 g) walnuts, chopped
4 oz (100 g) cheese, grated
salt and pepper

Pre-heat the oven to 180°C/350°F/Gas 4. Chop off some of the broccoli stalks and divide the broccoli into florets. Microwave, steam or boil for a few minutes – until starting to become tender, but still with some 'bite'. Meanwhile fry the mushrooms and garlic in the oil until starting to colour. Mix the broccoli and mushrooms together, season, and place in a large ovenproof dish. Spoon the cheese sauce over. Mix together the breadcrumbs, walnuts and cheese and sprinkle over the top of the dish. Cook in the pre-heated oven for about 40 minutes until brown on top.

Fennel gratin

Serves 8–10 (or 20 as part of a buffet)

    2 × 16 oz (2 × 400 g) cans chopped tomatoes
    4 cloves garlic, crushed
    4 tablespoons (60 ml) olive oil
    fresh basil leaves, shredded
    salt and pepper
    6 fennel bulbs, each sliced into 4
    3 oz (75 g) fresh breadcrumbs
    2 oz (50 g) grated Parmesan

First make a tomato sauce by cooking the tomatoes, garlic, oil and basil for 20 minutes. Season. Meanwhile, cook the fennel in boiling water for 15 minutes. Pre-heat the oven to 200°C/400°F/Gas 6. Put a thin layer of tomato sauce in a large ovenproof dish and then layer the fennel into this, covering with tomato sauce. Mix together the breadcrumbs and Parmesan and sprinkle over the dish. Cook in the pre-heated oven for 20–30 minutes until brown.

Mayonnaise

This is how our French friends make mayonnaise, and I have always found it to be a foolproof recipe. Don't worry that it looks a murky brown colour at the beginning – it does take on a lighter hue when the lemon juice and vinegar are added. It has a delicious fresh, tangy taste and will keep for a few days in the refrigerator.

    2 egg yolks
    1 teaspoon (5 ml) French mustard
    pinch of sugar
    salt and pepper
    10 fl oz (250 ml) olive or sunflower oil
    1 tablespoon (15 ml) lemon juice
    1 tablespoon (15 ml) white wine vinegar

Whisk the egg yolks with the mustard, sugar and seasoning. Whisk while slowly adding the oil. When thick, whisk in the lemon juice and vinegar.

Mediterranean pasta salad
Serves 10 (or 20 as part of a buffet)

This is an extremely popular recipe in our household. Not only is it included in buffets when we are entertaining, but it is an integral part of our summer meals. It goes particularly well with grilled or barbecued meats and it also makes a regular appearance at Sunday lunchtime during the summer months.

> 1 lb 4 oz (500 g) bag of pasta bows
> 4 tablespoons (60 ml) olive oil
> 1 tablespoon (15 ml) wine vinegar
> 1 tablespoon (15 ml) tomato purée
> 1 tablespoon (15 ml) red pesto
> small jar of sun-dried tomatoes in oil
> handful of pitted black olives, halved (optional)
> few shredded fresh basil leaves
> salt and pepper

Cook the pasta bows until 'al dente', and drain. Meanwhile mix together the oil, vinegar, tomato purée and red pesto. Season well. If the sun-dried tomatoes are whole, cut them up into small pieces. Now mix the pasta, dressing, sun-dried tomatoes and olives (if using) together and top with basil leaves. This salad can be made the day before you need it.

Coleslaw
Serves 10 (or 20 as part of a buffet)

Again this is a very firm family favourite when it comes to salads. My mother is particularly keen on this – although on the whole she is not a great coleslaw fan! I'm not sure whether it is the celeriac or the apple, or the combination of both, but it is the best coleslaw recipe I have come up with. Do try it – I'm sure you will be impressed with its fresh taste.

8 oz (200 g) celeriac, shredded
8 oz (200 g) white cabbage, shredded
8 oz (200 g) carrots, shredded
1 apple, coarsely grated
5 fl oz (125 ml) soured cream
2 cloves garlic, crushed
2 tablespoons (30 ml) mayonnaise
2 tablespoons (30 ml) salad cream
1 tablespoon (15 ml) white wine vinegar
1 tablespoon (15 ml) lemon juice
salt and pepper

Mix together the celeriac, white cabbage, carrot and apple. Now mix the rest of the ingredients together, seasoning well. Stir everything together and chill if possible. This is another salad that can be made the day before you wish to use it.

Brown rice and lentil salad
Serves 10 (or 20 as part of a buffet)

During the winter months this is a salad that can be found most weeks in our fridge! We serve it as an alternative to potatoes with grilled meats and fish, but it is also often used as a main course, when I serve it with a garlic or salsa sauce. I always find it amazing that something that is so healthy – and quick to make – can taste so good!

8 oz (200 g) green lentils
8 oz (200 g) brown rice
4 carrots, roughly grated
4 oz (100 g) pumpkin seeds
4 tablespoons (60 ml) olive oil
2 tablespoons (30 ml) lemon juice
2 cloves garlic, crushed
1 tablespoon (15 ml) caster sugar
2 tablespoons (30 ml) chopped fresh parsley
salt and pepper

Mix together the lentils and rice, stir in 1½ pints (750 ml) boiling water, cover and cook until tender, but not mushy. Drain if necessary, and leave to cool. Add the carrots and pumpkin seeds. Stir or shake the rest of the ingredients together and mix into the lentils and rice. Can be made the day before serving.

Three bean salad

Serves 10 (or 20 as part of a buffet)

2 × 16 oz (2 × 400 g) cans red kidney beans,
  drained
16 oz (400 g) can cannellini beans, drained
16 oz (400 g) can borlotti beans, drained
3 tablespoons (45 ml) olive oil
juice of 1 lemon
1 teaspoon (5 ml) French mustard
salt and pepper

Mix together the beans and then stir or shake the rest of
the ingredients together. Season well. Now stir everything together. (Handle the beans gently, as canned
beans can sometimes fall apart if roughly treated.) This
salad keeps well overnight.

Green salad
Serves 10 (or 20 as part of a buffet)

large bag of mixed salad leaves
4 celery sticks, sliced
½ a cucumber, thinly sliced
1 green pepper, chopped
4 tablespoons (60 ml) olive oil
2 tablespoons (30 ml) white wine vinegar
1 tablespoon (15 ml) medium dry sherry
1 tablespoon (15 ml) caster sugar
1 teaspoon (5 ml) Worcestershire sauce
1 clove garlic, crushed
pinch of mixed herbs
pinch of paprika
salt and pepper

Put the salad ingredients into a bowl. Stir or shake the rest of the ingredients and stir into the salad. This should be done immediately before serving.

Carrot and nut salad
Serves 10 (or 20 as part of a buffet)

2 lb (800 g) carrots, grated
2 oz (50 g) sunflower seeds
4 oz (100 g) unsalted cashew nuts
4 oz (100 g) raisins
6 tablespoons (90 ml) olive oil
4 tablespoons (60 ml) orange juice
1 tablespoon (15 ml) white wine vinegar
2 tablespoons (30 ml) fresh parsley, chopped
salt and pepper

Mix together the carrots, sunflower seeds, cashews and raisins. Stir or shake together the rest of the ingredients and then mix thoroughly into the salad. This can all be done the day before you wish to serve the salad.

Peperonata

Serves 10 (or 20 as part of a buffet)

2 onions, chopped
2 cloves garlic, crushed
6 peppers, sliced
4 celery stalks, diced
5 fl oz (125 ml) olive oil
2 × 16 oz (400 g) cans chopped tomatoes
salt and pepper

Fry the onion, garlic, peppers and celery in the oil until starting to colour (you will probably need to do this in batches) and remove to a large saucepan or flameproof casserole dish. Add the tomatoes and bring to the boil. Lower the heat and simmer for 30 minutes until the vegetables are soft. Season, and serve hot or cold.

Broad beans with mint

Serves 10 (or 20 as part of a buffet)

2 lb (800 g) broad beans
3 tablespoons (45 ml) fresh chopped mint
2 cloves garlic, crushed
5 fl oz (125 ml) olive oil
juice of 2 lemons
black pepper

Boil, steam or microwave the broad beans. Drain and mix with the other ingredients. Cool and serve.

Leeks in lemon and mustard vinaigrette
Serves 10 (or 20 as part of a buffet)

    6 lb (2.4 kg) leeks, sliced
    5 fl oz (125 ml) olive oil
    2 tablespoons (30 ml) balsamic vinegar
    2 tablespoons (30 ml) wholegrain mustard
    juice and grated rind of 1 lemon
    salt and pepper

Boil, steam or microwave the leeks until tender. Drain, and while still hot, mix together the other ingredients and stir into the leeks. Season well and leave to cool. Serve cold (but not chilled).

Tiramisu
Serves 10 (or 20 as part of a buffet)

A very fashionable dish – it is extremely good, and very quick and easy to make.

    30 sponge fingers
    12 fl oz (300 ml) strong black coffee
    3 tablespoons (45 ml) Kahlua or other coffee liqueur
    3 egg yolks
    3 tablespoons (45 ml) caster sugar
    1 teaspoon (5 ml) vanilla essence
    1 lb (400 g) mascarpone cheese
    cocoa powder, for dusting

Dip 10 of the sponge fingers into a mixture of the coffee and Kahlua. Lay in a serving dish. Beat together the egg yolks, sugar and vanilla essence. Add the mascarpone and mix well. Put a layer of this over the biscuits. Add another layer of biscuits and mascarpone mixture. Repeat. Dust with cocoa powder and chill for 2 hours before serving.

9 Anniversaries

These are important occasions – not to be forgotten! As with birthdays, it is not always possible to take your loved one out for a meal – but who cares if they're being cooked a lovely meal anyway? I think that the setting for these meals is important, and this is where children can come in useful as they get older – in my opinion all parents should teach their children how to decorate and lay up a table. It is while we are young that we are at our most creative, and children can often come up with artful ways to decorate the table – maybe it is all those hours spent watching *Blue Peter*! Certainly, anniversaries should be the one time that the spouse who doesn't normally cook gives it their best shot. (It's the least you can do – and really cooking isn't witchcraft! Even kids can do it.)

I give here some of our tried and trusty recipes that are really foolproof, yet special enough for such an important occasion. I also give two examples of very special menus for very rare occasions – a silver wedding and a golden wedding anniversary.

Suggested menus
(Recipes are given in the order shown below)

Family anniversary dinner
Asparagus and cheat's hollandaise

Roasted salmon
New potatoes (see page 106)
Broccoli with anchovy butter (see page 68)

Fruit puffs

Drinks
Sparkling wine
Soft drinks

Silver anniversary (buffet)
Fish platter

Roast ham
Raisin sauce
Selection of salads

Selection of desserts and cheeses

Drinks
Red and white wine
Sparkling wine for toasts
Soft drinks

Golden anniversary (seated)
Carrot and coriander soup

Curried chicken casserole with apricots
Selection of vegetables or salads
Rice

Mango and orange cheesecake (see page 184)

Drinks
Red and white wine
Sparkling wine for toasts
Soft drinks

Other suggested recipes
Prawns in cocktail sauce
Crusted fish
Coq au vin
Roast pheasant
Game casserole
Pork with rich mustardy cream sauce
Duck with blackcurrant sauce
Seville sauce (for duck)
Anna potatoes
Broccoli gratin
Creamed celeriac
Potted cheese

Asparagus
Serves 4 as a starter

1½–2 lb (600–800 g) asparagus
melted butter or hollandaise sauce

Wash the asparagus spears to ensure all grit is removed –
this is especially important if you have picked them
yourself. Snap or cut off the woody stem. (If you snap it
off, you ensure that all the inedible part is being
removed.) Boil, steam or microwave until the stems are
tender – keep testing, as you do not want to overcook
them. Cooking can take anything from 6–16 minutes.
Serve with butter or hollandaise sauce spread over the
bud ends.

Cheat's hollandaise
Serves 4–6

Hollandaise is a sauce that can go wrong. This is my
answer. I can only make it in a microwave – but on the
other hand it has never gone wrong.

4 oz (100 g) butter
2 egg yolks
1 tablespoon (15 ml) lemon juice
½ teaspoon (2.5 ml) mustard powder
2 tablespoons (30 ml) crème fraîche
pinch of salt

Melt the butter in a microwave for 2 minutes. Meanwhile,
beat the rest of the ingredients together. When the butter
is hot, stir in the rest of the ingredients. Put back into the
microwave and cook for 15 seconds. Stir well. Repeat
until the sauce has thickened – stop as soon as it has. (It
should be like a thin custard – I have a 650w microwave
and it usually takes 45 seconds in total.)

Roasted salmon
Serves 4

This was one of the first dishes I ever made for a dinner party. I wanted something that couldn't go wrong and that is why it is still a strong favourite.

> 4 salmon steaks
> melted butter
> sprigs of tarragon
> 2 tablespoons (30 ml) white wine
> salt and pepper

Pre-heat the oven to 180°C/350°F/Gas 4. Take a sheet of foil and brush it with butter. Place it in a shallow baking tin and place the salmon steaks on top. Brush the steaks with butter and put a small sprig of tarragon on each steak. Drizzle the wine over the salmon and season. Wrap the foil round loosely, and cook in the pre-heated oven for 20 minutes. Serve hot or cold.

Fruit puffs
Serves 4

> 8 oz (200 g) puff pastry
> fresh fruit of your choice (e.g. sliced apple,
>   strawberries, blackcurrants or raspberries)
> 1 tablespoon (15 ml) marmalade or jam
> 1 tablespoon (15 ml) brandy
> 1 tablespoon (15 ml) caster sugar
> beaten egg to glaze

Pre-heat the oven to 230°C/450°F/Gas 8. Roll out the pastry and cut into 4 oval shapes. Into the middle of each, place your chosen fruit, leaving a border around the edge. Melt the jam and brandy together and use to glaze the fruit. Sprinkle with the sugar. Glaze the pastry edges with the egg. Cook in the pre-heated oven for 10–12 minutes until the pastry is risen and brown.

Fish platter
Serves 10 (or 20 as part of a buffet)

> prawnnaise (see next recipe)
> prawns in cocktail sauce
> 1 lb (400 g) head-on prawns
> 8 oz (200 g) smoked salmon

On a large serving platter, arrange 2 bowls and fill with the prawnnaise and prawns in cocktail sauce. In the middle of the platter lay out the head-on prawns. Cut the smoked salmon into small strips, roll them up, and put these salmon rolls around the edge of the platter.

Prawnnaise
Serves 8-10 (or 20 as part of a buffet)

This is a delicious alternative to prawns in cocktail sauce and is fast growing in popularity – with most super-markets now making their own. It is extremely easy to make, however, and of course is much cheaper when any decent quantity is needed.

> 1 pint (500 ml) mayonnaise
> 10 fl oz (250 ml) single cream
> juice of 1 lemon
> 4 cloves garlic, crushed
> 1 lb (400 g) cooked, peeled prawns
> salt and pepper

Combine all the ingredients and season well.

Roasted glazed ham

This is an essential part of Christmas for us, but also an extremely useful dish on many entertaining occasions. The beauty of a ham is not only that you can feed large numbers of people very easily, but also that it keeps well and there are so many ways in which you can use leftovers – in salads, sandwiches, with egg and chips, in pasta dishes or on pizzas, to name just a few. Ask the butcher for guidance on how many servings you can expect from the joint you are buying.

> ham joint
> 5 fl oz (125 ml) apple juice or cider
> bay leaf
> a few peppercorns
> cloves
> 3 tablespoons (45 ml) Seville marmalade
> 3 tablespoons (45 ml) runny honey
> 1 tablespoon (15 ml) mustard

Put the ham in a large saucepan with the apple juice, bay leaf and peppercorns. Add just enough water to cover. Bring to the boil and draw off the scum that forms on the water. Cover and simmer. The ham will need a total cooking time of 20 minutes per pound plus 20 minutes. Simmer for half the cooking time. Pre-heat the oven to 180°C/350°F/Gas 4. Drain and remove the rind from the ham. Score the fat into diamonds and stud with cloves. Roast in the pre-heated oven until 30 minutes before cooking time is up. Mix the marmalade, honey and mustard together. Glaze the ham with half the mixture and roast for another 15 minutes before repeating with the rest of the mixture. When the cooking time is up, remove from the oven and leave to cool.

Raisin sauce
Serves 8–10

This is a very sweet sauce and you will only want a touch
with your ham, but it does set it off nicely.

2 oz (50 g) soft dark brown sugar
pinch of English mustard
1 tablespoon (15 ml) cornflour
3 oz (75 g) raisins
grated rind and juice of an orange
8 fl oz (200 ml) water

Mix together the sugar, mustard and cornflour. Blend in
the rest of the ingredients and cook over a gentle heat for
10 minutes until you have a syrupy sauce.

Carrot and coriander soup
Serves 6–8

1½ lb (600 g) carrots, chopped
1 medium-sized potato, chopped
1 large onion, chopped
2 oz (50 g) butter
1½ pints (750 ml) vegetable stock
sprinkling of ground coriander
1 tablespoon (15 ml) cornflour
5 fl oz (125 ml) milk
4 tablespoons (60 ml) single cream
1 tablespoon (15 ml) chopped fresh coriander
salt and pepper

Fry the vegetables in the butter until soft, but not browning. Add the stock and ground coriander and bring to the
boil, then cover and simmer for 40–45 minutes until the
vegetables are very soft. Blend or purée and return to the
heat. Blend the cornflour with some of the milk and add
with the rest of the milk to the pan. Remove from the heat
and stir in the cream and chopped coriander.

Curried chicken casserole with apricots
Serves 6–8

   6 large chicken breasts
   4 tablespoons (60 ml) olive oil
   2 onions, chopped
   2 cloves garlic, crushed
   1 teaspoon (5 ml) ginger purée
   2–3 tablespoons (30–40 ml) curry paste
   10 fl oz (250 ml) chicken stock
   16 fl oz (400 ml) canned coconut milk
   2 × 16 oz (2 × 400 g) cans apricots, drained
   3–4 tablespoons (45–60 ml) double cream

Pre-heat the oven to 170°C/325°F/Gas 3. Cut each chicken breast into 4 pieces. Fry the chicken in oil just long enough to colour the meat, and then transfer to a large casserole dish. Fry the onions, garlic and ginger for 10 minutes until soft and brown. Add the curry paste and fry for 1 minute. Add the stock and coconut milk. Bring to the boil and then transfer to a casserole dish. Cook in the pre-heated oven for 1 hour. Add the apricots and cream and heat through. Serve with rice.

Prawns in cocktail sauce
Serves 8–10 (or 20 as part of a buffet)

This must be one of the most popular of starters. It can be served on a bed of lettuce, and is sometimes served with avocado pears. I have to admit that at a very young age, when I first started going out to restaurants, it was the starter I always chose. In those days I then proceeded to extricate the prawns and only ate the cocktail sauce – you see, I didn't like prawns!

10 fl oz (250 ml) mayonnaise
10 fl oz (250 ml) tomato ketchup
10 fl oz (250 ml) single cream
juice of ½ a lemon
dash of Worcestershire sauce
1 lb (400 g) cooked, peeled prawns
salt and pepper

Mix together all the ingredients and season to taste.

Crusted fish
Serves 4

2 tablespoons (30 ml) whole mixed peppercorns, crushed
1 tablespoon (15 ml) plain flour
1 tablespoon (15 ml) dried wholemeal breadcrumbs
pinch of paprika
4 × 8 oz (4 × 200 g) fresh cod fillets
6 tablespoons (90 ml) olive oil
2 cloves garlic, crushed
1 tablespoon (15 ml) wholegrain mustard
grated rind and juice of 1 lemon
grated rind and juice of 1 lime
chopped fresh coriander, basil or mint

Pre-heat the oven to 180°C/350°F/Gas 4. In a plastic bag, mix the crushed peppercorns, flour, breadcrumbs and paprika. Place each fillet into the bag and coat with the breadcrumb mixture. Lay on a baking sheet. Sprinkle any remaining mixture over the cod fillets. Bake in the pre-heated oven for 20 minutes. To serve, mix the rest of the ingredients, heat through, and pour over and around the fish.

Coq au vin
Serves 4

This has to be one of our all-time favourites. I must admit, however, that we are continually changing the recipe in our quest to find the ultimate coq au vin. This is our current favourite – the items of prime importance in this dish are the chicken and the wine used. Do pay out more and get a decent bird and bottle – it really does make a difference. On the subject of cooking with wine, my advice is never to use a wine for cooking that you wouldn't personally drink – you are unlikely to be happy with the resulting dish. If Andy is cooking this he will probably use a claret – while I prefer something a little fruitier, such as a Beaujolais. Since the cook gets to slurp some of the wine that has been opened to cook with, choose the wine you are happiest with!

3½ lb (1.4 kg) corn-fed chicken, jointed
paprika
salt and pepper
1 tablespoon (15 ml) olive oil
2 oz (50 g) butter
4 oz (100 g) smoked streaky bacon, cubed (optional)
4 shallots, quartered, or 16 pickling onions
4 cloves garlic, crushed
1 tablespoon (15 ml) freeze-dried tarragon or a sprig
    of fresh tarragon
1 pint (500 ml) red wine
4 plum tomatoes, quartered, or a 7 oz (200 g) can
    chopped tomatoes
1 tablespoon (15 ml) tomato purée

Pre-heat the oven to 180°C/350°F/Gas 4. Season the chicken with paprika, salt and pepper. Fry each piece in the oil and butter until brown. Transfer the chicken to a large casserole dish. Fry the bacon, shallots and garlic until brown and add to the casserole. Stir in the rest of the ingredients. Cover the casserole and cook in the pre-heated oven for 1–2 hours.

You will notice that I have introduced the use of plum tomatoes in this recipe. These appeared in our local supermarket about a year ago. Although still not as tasty as the tomatoes you will find if you are cooking on holiday in Italy or France, the flavour is definitely superior to those tomatoes usually available to us. If you cannot get them, do substitute canned tomatoes as opposed to fresh tomatoes.

Roast pheasant
Serves 4

This is the French way of roasting pheasant. The sherry ensures that the meat stays moist while cooking.

    brace of pheasant, dressed with bacon
    2 oz (50 g) butter
    2 shallots, quartered
    1 bay leaf
    knob of butter for cooking
    glass of medium dry sherry

Pre-heat the oven to 220°C/425°F/Gas 7. Smear the 2 oz (50 g) butter over the pheasants and place with the shallots and bay leaf in a small roasting dish. Add the knob of butter and pour the sherry over the birds and into the dish. Roast in the pre-heated oven for 10 minutes, then reduce the heat to 180°C/350°F/Gas 4 for a further 30–40 minutes. Pierce birds – if the juices run clear they are done.

Game casserole
Serves 4

This is a great favourite in the winter months. Where we live we are blessed with many game butchers, but some supermarkets now sell mixed portions of game, which are ideal for this dish. You can also make it using any game bird or venison.

> 1 lb (400 g) mixed game, diced
> 2 cloves garlic, crushed
> 10 fl oz (250 ml) red wine
> 5 fl oz (125 ml) olive oil
> salt and pepper
> 1 shallot, finely chopped
> 2 carrots, diced
> 1 oz (25 g) butter
> 2 tablespoons (30 ml) plain flour
> 8 fl oz (200 ml) rich beef stock
> bay leaf
> sprig of rosemary
> 12 button mushrooms
> cornflour (optional)

Marinade the game in the garlic, wine, olive oil and salt and pepper overnight. Pre-heat the oven to 170°C/325°F/ Gas 3. Fry the shallot and carrots in the butter until soft. stir in flour and cook for 1 minute. Add the stock and stir while it thickens. Put into a casserole dish with the rest of the ingredients. Cook in the pre-heated oven for 1½–2 hours. Look at it 30 minutes before the cooking time is up, and decide whether you wish to thicken the liquid with cornflour.

Pork with rich mustardy cream sauce
Serves 4

4 pork loin chops
1 oz (25 g) butter
5 fl oz (125 ml) dry white wine
1 tablespoon (15 ml) fresh chopped thyme
5 fl oz (125 ml) crème fraîche
2 tablespoons (30 ml) Dijon mustard
salt and pepper

Fry the chops in the butter until they are brown and the meat is cooked (about 15 minutes). Add the wine and thyme to the pan and bring to the boil. Turn the heat down and add the crème fraîche and Dijon mustard. Season. Simmer for 2 minutes, to let the sauce thicken, and heat through before serving.

Duck with blackcurrant sauce
Serves 4

Duck has become a very fashionable meat over the last few years, and this sauce is very popular (I also make a similar sauce with blackberries). However, for those who prefer it I also give the recipe for an orange sauce, which is the more traditional accompaniment.

2 duck breasts
1 tablespoon (15 ml) olive oil
2 shallots, finely chopped
8 fl oz (200 ml) wine
2 teaspoons (10 ml) raspberry or wine vinegar
4 oz (100 g) fresh blackcurrants
2 tablespoons (30 ml) blackcurrant preserve
salt and pepper
cornflour or arrowroot (optional)
knob of butter

Prick the skin of the duck several times, then fry in the oil. Cook for 12 minutes, skin side down, and then turn over and cook for another 5 minutes. Put in a warm place, covered with foil, to rest. Tip off half of the fat from the pan and add the shallots, cook until soft, and then add the rest of the ingredients except the cornflour and butter. Bring to the boil and simmer for a few minutes until you have a sauce of the consistency that you like (you can thicken it with cornflour or arrowroot if you wish). Beat in the knob of butter and season. Slice the duck breast thinly and serve with the sauce.

Seville sauce (for duck)
Serves 4

The traditional accompaniment for duck has always been orange sauce, so for the traditionalists I have included this recipe.

> 3 tablespoons (45 ml) Seville marmalade
> juice of 1 lemon
> 1 tablespoon (15 ml) soft dark brown sugar
> 1 tablespoon (15 ml) vinegar
> 2 tablespoons (30 ml) brandy
> salt and pepper

Heat all the ingredients together. Taste and adjust the seasoning to suit.

Anna potatoes
Serves 4

> 1 oz (25 g) butter, melted
> 1 lb (400 g) potatoes, thinly sliced
> grated rind and juice of ½ a lemon
> salt and pepper

Pre-heat the oven to 180°C/350°F/Gas 4. Line a 7 in (18 cm) cake tin with baking parchment. Brush with melted butter and layer the potatoes into the tin, brushing with more butter and sprinkling with the lemon rind, salt and pepper as you build up the layers. Pour the lemon juice over the potatoes, cover tightly with foil, and cook in the pre-heated oven for 1–1¼ hours until the potatoes are tender. Put under a hot grill for a few minutes to brown. Remove the tin and the paper, and serve cut into wedges.

Broccoli gratin
Serves 4

> 1 lb (400 g) broccoli
> 14 oz (400 g) can chopped tomatoes
> 2 tablespoons (30 ml) tomato purée
> 2 teaspoons (10 ml) red pesto
> ½ an 8 fl oz (200 ml) carton of crème fraîche
> 1 oz (25 g) fresh breadcrumbs
> 2 oz (50 g) cheese, grated
> salt and pepper

Pre-heat the oven to 180°C/350°F/Gas 4. Chop off some of the broccoli stalks and divide the broccoli into florets. Microwave, steam or boil for a few minutes so that they are half-cooked, but still have some 'bite'. Spread one third of the can of the tomatoes over the bottom of a gratin dish. Mix the rest of the can with the tomato purée and red pesto. Drain the broccoli and layer into the dish. Season well. Spoon the tomato mixture over the broccoli and then top with crème fraîche. Mix together the breadcrumbs and cheese, and sprinkle over the dish. Bake in the pre-heated oven for 40–50 minutes, until brown on top.

Creamed celeriac
Serves 4

> 1 lb (400 g) celeriac, cubed
> 2 tablespoons (30 ml) single or double cream
> salt and pepper

Microwave or boil the celeriac until very tender. Drain, then mash or purée. Stir in the cream and season well.

Potted cheese
Serves 4

We are all lovers of good cheese in my family. This is a particular favourite. We like it made with a particularly good mature Cheddar, but it can also be made with blue cheese (when I usually substitute port for the sherry) or a good Cheshire.

8 oz (200 g) grated strong-flavoured cheese
4 oz (100 g) softened butter
4 tablespoons (60 ml) medium dry sherry
pinch of mace
pinch of mustard powder
salt and pepper

Mix all the ingredients together. Chill until ready to serve.

10 60th/65th Birthdays – Retirement Parties

While the coming of age/engagement parties in Chapter 2 were for the younger generation, this chapter is for the 'recycled teenagers' – as they call them in the States. As I get older – and I am still in my 30s – I realize that essentially you don't change as you get older. You may achieve a more mature outlook on life (as you gain experience), but underneath you stay the same person you were at 20, and I believe that even when you reach the status of an 'OAP' you are not able to identify with actually having become a 'golden oldie'!

Thus it can come as a great shock to people when they reach retirement age – the years just seem to slip by faster, the older you get. However, it is a time to start putting yourself first and making the most

out of life and your new leisure time. When my mother reached her 60th birthday it was gratifying to hear her say at her party that if she'd known it was going to be this much fun she'd have done it ten years earlier! She also celebrated by taking a trip on the Orient Express and going hot-air ballooning for the first time – who said life begins at 40!

So, just as it's important to mark the start of your adult life, I think it is also important to mark the start of a new era – that of less work and more play!

When catering for this type of party – although it will be an affair of mixed age groups – you will find on the whole that less will get eaten and drunk than you expect. People do slow down as they get older. I was amazed to find that I still had a full case of wine left after my mother's party – and masses of canned beers and lagers.

We chose to have a buffet at home, but another popular option is to have a seated meal in a hired hall. I think that decorations are very important, and for my mother's do, Andy had spent twelve hours the previous day putting up the decorations. We chose yellow and white as the theme colours, and by hanging alternate sheets of coloured crêpe paper to cover both the ceiling and the walls, managed to create a tented marquee effect inside the house. We completed the party atmosphere by having masses of yellow and white balloons (of various sizes and shapes) with ribbons and bows adorning every available corner and at points along the walls. Mother (who had been nonplussed when I tried to describe what we were going to do) was very impressed with the final result. We also had plenty of flowers, and with the flowers that continued to arrive throughout the day and evening, the house looked really wonderful.

We felt it was a real shame to dismantle the decorations afterwards – but they didn't go to waste, as my mother and her friend Kath gathered all the balloons and crêpe paper together and took them all off to a local primary school – where they were gratefully received. So now you know what to do with the decorations after your party!

NB: As I was very pregnant at the time of the party it was imperative that I didn't overload myself with work. I therefore felt no guilt at all in buying in some platters already made up from a supermarket deli. My mother and I made up the coronation chicken and the salads, but I bought in the salmon and the profiteroles. So on the day I only had to finish off the two desserts I had already started.

We also had a lunchtime buffet – and the work for this was done by Andy, my brother and his wife – my mother and I went off to the hairdresser's to have our hair and nails done!

So don't feel guilty about not doing everything yourself – it's the finished effect that counts!

Mother's 60th birthday party menu
(Recipes are given in the order shown below)

Dips and crudités (see pages 34-6)
Oriental platter from supermarket deli

Poached dressed salmon
Coronation chicken (see page 94)
Cold meats platter
Selection of salads

Raspberry vacherin
Mango and orange cheesecake
Profiteroles with chocolate sauce
Selection of cheeses

Birthday cake

Drinks
Red and white wine
Pink punch
Iced tea
Beers and lagers
Champagne with the cake

Poached dressed salmon
Serves 14 (or 20 as part of a buffet)

I think that you have to be quite brave to attempt this dish, but like most things, when you actually attempt it, it is quite easy. It is a great way of saving money, as although you can now obtain dressed salmon at a number of supermarkets (order it through the deli) it is of course much cheaper to do it yourself. You do need a bit of time – it can be fiddly taking the skin off and the bones out – but do not be tempted to leave these jobs to your guests, as it greatly reduces the pleasure of the dish if you have to negotiate the bones.

1 × 6 lb (2.4 kg) salmon, cleaned and gills removed
4 fl oz (100 ml) white wine vinegar
8 pints (4 litres) water
3 bay leaves
1 onion, sliced
1 carrot, sliced
12 black whole peppercorns
few sprigs of parsley

To decorate
peeled prawns
sliced cucumber
chopped parsley
made-up packet of aspic jelly

Put the salmon and all the other ingredients into a fish kettle and poach the fish very gently (not at a fast simmer). This size fish should take about 30 minutes – it is cooked when the dorsal fin comes away easily. Cool overnight in the liquid. Next day, carefully take the fish from the liquid. Remove the head and tail (but reserve for serving). Carefully skin the fish. Split the fish and remove the bones. Place on a serving dish and reassemble the two sides of salmon. Remove the eye from the head and replace the head. Replace the tail. Put a line of prawns down the middle of the salmon, interspersed with parsley. Put a line of cucumber slices down each side of the salmon. Now brush with aspic jelly and leave to set.

NB: It is possible to hire fish kettles from some shops that sell cookery utensils.

Raspberry vacherin
Serves 8–12

This is the second of two recipes that I developed specially for my mother's birthday bash. (It took me only two attempts to get it right.) It has also proved very popular, and as it's so easy to make I can see it becoming a popular choice when we are entertaining.

On the night of my mother's birthday this dessert had barely reached the table before I had people queuing up for it!

    4 egg-whites, beaten
    8 oz (200 g) caster sugar
    1 tablespoon (15 ml) cornflour, sieved
    2 oz (50 g) dark cooking chocolate
    1 lb (400 g) raspberries
    1 tablespoon (15 ml) icing sugar, sieved
    4 tablespoons (60 ml) raspberry jam
    2 tablespoons (30 ml) cassis (optional)
    1 sachet gelatine
    1 pint (500 ml) whipping cream, whipped
    10 fl oz (250 ml) double cream, beaten
    2 oz (50 g) toasted, flaked almonds

Pre-heat the oven to its lowest setting. To the stiffly beaten egg-whites, add half the caster sugar and beat until glossy. Gently fold in the rest of the caster sugar and the sieved cornflour. Using the bottom of a 9 inch (23 cm) springform cake tin, draw two circles on some non-stick baking parchment. Spread the meringue in those circles so that you have 2 rounds of meringue that will eventually fit inside the cake tin. Level the circles and cook in the pre-heated oven for 2–2½ hours, until completely dry. These can be made in advance and kept in an airtight container.

On the day before you wish to serve your raspberry vacherin, put one meringue circle in the base of your 9 inch (23 cm) springform tin, melt the chocolate and pour over the meringue. Reserve half of the raspberries and sieve the rest into a bowl. Mix in the sieved icing sugar. Melt the raspberry jam and add with the cassis (if using) to the sieved raspberries. Spread or pour 2 tablespoons of the mixture over the chocolate. Mix 2 tablespoons with the reserved raspberries. Now add the remaining mixture to the whipped cream.

Make up the gelatine as directed on the packet, but using 3 tablespoons of water. Stir the dissolved gelatine into the raspberry and cream mixture. Spread this mixture over the meringue. Now top with the other meringue circle. Chill until set (I like to leave it overnight). To decorate, carefully unmould the vacherin and spread the beaten double cream around the edges. Using your fingers or a flat knife gently press the almonds over the cream. Top with the reserved raspberries in raspberry jam and cassis mixture.

Mango and orange cheesecake
Serves 8–12

This is one of the recipes that I recently concocted for my mother's 60th birthday celebrations. It took me three attempts to come up with a recipe that I was happy with, but this is all set now to become a firm family favourite. Although I have used mango and orange here, I can see no reason why other fruits cannot be used – other versions I intend to try will be raspberry and redcurrants, lemon and lime and gooseberry and stem ginger!

8 oz (200 g) curd cheese
1 lb 4 oz (500 g) creamy fromage frais
2 oz (50 g) caster sugar
16 oz (400 g) can mango slices in syrup
grated rind and 2 tablespoons (30 ml) juice from an
    orange
2–3 sachets (1 oz/25 g) gelatine
5 fl oz (125 ml) double cream, whipped
4 oz (100 g) wholemeal digestive biscuits, crushed
2 oz (50 g) butter, melted
1 teaspoon (5 ml) arrowroot
12 oz (300 g) can mandarin segments, drained
whipping cream to decorate

Mix together the curd cheese, fromage frais and sugar. Stir until smooth. Blend the mango with 2 tablespoons of the syrup from the can. Reserve 2 tablespoons of the purée and mix the rest, with the grated orange rind, into the cheesecake mixture. Following the instructions on the gelatine packet, make up with 4 tablespoons of hot water. Mix the dissolved gelatine into the cheesecake mixture and stir well. Blend in the whipped cream. Line a 2 lb (800 g) loaf tin with baking parchment and fill with the cheesecake mixture. Chill for 1 hour. Mix the biscuit crumbs and melted butter and cover the cheesecake. Chill until set.

Up to this stage, everything can be done the day before you wish to serve the cheesecake. Blend the reserved purée with 2 tablespoons (30 ml) orange juice and the arrowroot and bring to the boil, stirring until smooth and thick. Leave to cool. Invert the cheesecake on to a serving dish and carefully remove the paper. Arrange the mandarin segments on top and spoon the mango purée over, covering the top. Decorate with whipped cream around the base.

Profiteroles
Serves 10 (or 20 as part of a buffet)

Choux pastry
2½ oz (60 g) butter or soft margarine
8 fl oz (200 ml) water
4 oz (100 g) plain flour
3 eggs, beaten

Filling
10 fl oz (250 ml) double cream

Pre-heat the oven to 220°C/425°F/Gas 7. Melt the fat in the water and bring to the boil. Remove from the heat and tip all the flour in together. Return to the heat and beat the paste into a smooth ball. Allow to cool a little, then gradually beat in the eggs. Either put into a piping bag and pipe small balls on to greased baking sheets, or place in small round heaps on the baking sheets (do not over-handle the pastry). This will make about 30–40 balls. Bake in the pre-heated oven for 20 minutes, until brown and well-risen. Make a hole in the side of each ball, and return to the oven for 5–10 minutes to dry out completely. Place on a wire rack to cool. When ready, beat the cream and, using a piping bag, fill each ball with cream (inject through the hole in the side). Serve with your chosen sauce.

Chocolate sauce
Serves 4–6

> 4 oz (100 g) good cooking chocolate
> knob of butter
> 2 tablespoons (30 ml) golden syrup
> 4 fl oz (100 ml) boiling water

Melt all the ingredients together and serve with profiteroles.

Fudge sauce
Serves 8–12

> 8 oz (200 g) soft dark brown sugar
> 6 oz (150 g) butter
> 10 fl oz (250 ml) double cream
> 1 teaspoon (5 ml) vanilla essence

Melt all the ingredients together and then boil for 5 minutes. Serve with profiteroles.

Celebration cake
Makes an 11 inch (28 cm) round cake

No celebration is complete without the cake. At long last I am revealing my recipe, which I have used for all the important cakes that have marked special occasions in our family. This has included weddings, christenings, and of course my mother's 60th. It is a really wonderful cake that stays moist for absolutely months. (I think this is due to the large amount of alcohol that goes into it!)

2½ lb (1 kg) mixed dried fruit
1¼ lb (500 g) stoned raisins, chopped
8 oz (200 g) candied peel, chopped
8 oz (200 g) glace cherries, chopped
4 tablespoons (60 ml) brandy
4 tablespoons (60 ml) Grand Marnier
1¼ lb (500 g) plain flour
pinch of salt
pinch of nutmeg
1 teaspoon (5 ml) mixed spice
1¼ lb (500 g) unsalted butter
1¼ lb (500 g) soft dark brown sugar
9 eggs, beaten
4 oz (100 g) flaked toasted almonds, crushed
1 tablespoon (15 ml) black treacle
4 oz (100 g) plain cooking chocolate, melted
grated rind of 1 lemon
grated rind of 1 orange

Start the night before you wish to bake the cake. Soak the fruit, peel and glace cherries in the alcohol. The smell in the morning is heavenly! Prepare your baking tin before you start to mix the cake. In our house this is one of Andy's jobs – I only have to lend him a finger when it comes to tying the brown paper around the outside of the tin. You need to line the cake tin on the inside with two layers of non-stick silicone paper, and also cut out two circles to place on top. Around the outside of the cake tin, tie a double thickness of thick brown paper – you can buy this at a newsagent's.

For the cake, pre-heat the oven to 140°C/275°F/Gas 1.

Sift the flour, salt, nutmeg and spice into a large bowl. Beat the butter and sugar together until light and fluffy. Now start to add the beaten eggs to the sugar and butter mixture, beating them in well and adding the odd table-spoon of flour to the mixture to stop it curdling. Then fold in the flour, followed by the rest of the ingredients. Carefully spoon the mixture into the prepared tin, trying to get it as level as possible. Cut a small hole in the middle of the greaseproof paper circles you have made for the top and put them on top of the mixture. Place a sheet of brown paper on the lowest rack in the oven and the tin on top of this. Bake in the pre-heated oven for $4^1/_2$–$5^1/_2$ hours. You will know it is ready when it is brown, has stopped 'sizzling', and when a warm skewer inserted into the cake comes out completely clean. Leave it to rest in the tin for 30 minutes and then turn it out on to a wire rack to cool. Remove the greaseproof paper. When completely cool, wrap in more greaseproof paper and foil. Make sure it is completely airtight. Leave for a few weeks and 'feed' the cake with brandy or Grand Marnier (by making little holes in it with a skewer and spooning the alcohol on to it to be absorbed).

Marzipanning the cake
To cover an 11 inch (28 cm) round cake

> $2^1/_2$ lb (1 kg) white marzipan
> 1 tablespoon (15 ml) apricot jam
> 1 tablespoon (15 ml) brandy

Cut one third of the marzipan off the block and roll out to cover the top of the cake. Now roll out the rest into strips to cover the sides of the cake. When you have cut them to the right size, melt the apricot jam and brandy together and use to brush the cake. Place the marzipan on top of the cake and then cover the sides. Flatten the edges, so that the cake is sealed. Leave for one day before icing the cake.

Royal icing
To cover an 11 inch (28 cm) round cake

I was much better at icing when I was at school. I can actually remember achieving a flat surface – something I seem incapable of now. However, there are plenty of ways of getting around this. I never bother with piping on cakes – I decorate mine with colourful ribbons around the side or lace (sometimes both), and for Christmas cakes I rough up the surface and have just one decoration in the middle, such as holly leaves and a bauble or single candle. Another alternative is to make a wavy pattern on the top. So even if you have no artistic qualities it is possible to give your cake an attractive finish.

3 egg-whites
1¼ lb (500 g) icing sugar, sifted
1 teaspoon (5 ml) glycerine

Lightly stir the egg-whites into the icing sugar and then whisk until the icing reaches the stiff peak stage. Stir in the glycerine – this ensures that the icing doesn't set rock hard! Spread the icing over the top and down the edges of the cake. Level the top of the cake and then with a clean comb, make wavy patterns over the top. Leave to set. Any remaining icing can be kept in a plastic bag to help stick decorations on to the cake.

Pink punch
Serves 6–8

1 pint (500 ml) cranberry juice
1 pint (500 ml) sparkling apple juice
1 pint (500 ml) freshly squeezed orange juice
1 orange, sliced
ice

Chill all the ingredients before using. Just before you are ready to serve, mix all the ingredients together in a jug or punch bowl. Use plenty of ice.

Iced tea
Serves 12

This is an excellent punch for hot summer evenings. Of course you can make an alcoholic version (commonly made with light and dark rum), but it is one of the nicest non-alcoholic drinks I have ever made.

12 English Breakfast teabags
6 tablespoons (90 ml) caster sugar
6 pints (3 litres) boiling water
24 sprigs of fresh mint
1 pint (500 ml) freshly squeezed orange juice
juice of 1 lime
juice of 1 lemon
1 orange, sliced
ice

Make up the tea with the teabags, caster sugar, boiling water and half the mint. Leave for 20 minutes and then remove the teabags and mint. Leave until completely cool and then add the orange, lime and lemon juice with the rest of the mint. Add the sliced orange and ice just before serving.

11 Christmas

Christmas comes but once a year . . .

For some that is quite enough – many people see Christmas as being too commercialized nowadays. However, I love it, complete with the sentimental claptrap that we get on the telly at this time of the year. I don't even get upset by the exploitation in the shops, which insist on stocking Christmas goodies as early as September.

Whenever I think of Christmas, I envisage the family gathered around the over-decorated tree, happily opening presents, a roaring log fire, the groaning table full of food, and of course . . . snow. Each year I predict a white Christmas, and it never comes . . . but there's always next year! Remember, the optimist leads a happier life than the pessimist.

In order that we see both sets of parents, Christmas nowadays revolves around a warming casserole on Christmas Eve (casseroles being the most versatile of dishes when because of weather/road conditions you never know what time people will be arriving). Then comes Christmas lunch with all the trimmings (which never changes, as our family like a traditional meal – never mind what the food pundits are saying is in fashion this year). On Boxing Day we usually have a rib of beef. After that we live on cold meats, cheese, pickles, etc. – except when we are expecting the other set of parents and assorted family/friends for lunch. That day I will cook a ham and make a trifle, and with a salad and some baked potatoes that will feed any number of people that turn up. I cook a large ham, as we are addicted to ham and chips in our house – and it's also useful for sandwich lunches or to go with baked potatoes or in pasta supper dishes.

I also keep a stock of mince pies and sausage rolls at hand for feeding the odd stray who turns up – as well as the ingredients for mulled wine, which we drink a lot at this time of year. I used to be very happy to buy mincemeat, a Christmas pudding and cake – there are many very good luxury ones for sale now. However, as I have become more organized, I have found that as long as I start in November I can easily fit the making of these goodies into my busy weekends. I do this for two reasons – first, the smell when they are cooking is heavenly and certainly brings the spirit of Christmas home, and second – even if I say it myself – they taste divine, much better than shop-bought ones can be. However, I still strongly believe that you should only attempt these goodies if you really do have the time. You will only have a good Christmas if you are feeling calm and unflustered. So don't try and do too much, and have . . . a very happy Christmas.

Suggested Christmas menus
(Recipes are given in the order shown below)

Christmas Eve
Rich beef casserole with prunes
Stir-fried celery and walnuts
Sherried potatoes
Swede and orange purée
French beans and flaked hazelnuts

Mincemeat parcels

Drinks
Red wine

Christmas Day
Christmas turkey
Pork, chestnut and orange stuffing
Bread sauce
Cranberry sauce
Roast potatoes (see page 102)
Brussels sprouts and chestnuts
Peas and carrots
Gravy (see page 101)

Christmas pudding
Rum sauce
Brandy butter

Drinks
Champagne
Red and white wine

Christmas buffet
Roasted glazed ham (see page 163)
Jacket potatoes (see page 59)
Selection of salads

Trifle

Drinks
Red and white wine
Beers and lager
Mulled wine
Pink Punch (see page 190)

Vegetarian Christmas dinner
Substitute stuffed nut roast and onion sauce for the
Christmas turkey and gravy.

Other suggested recipes
Lamb in red wine
Christmas cake
Homemade mincemeat

Rich beef casserole with prunes
Serves 6–8

This is a basic recipe for beef casserole. It can be adapted in many ways. I sometimes substitute Guinness for the red wine, or add redcurrant jelly instead of the prunes to enrich the sauce. You can vary the herbs that you use and even substitute venison for the beef. I have also substituted a country bramble wine and used it to cook rabbit – so it really is very versatile.

3 lb (1.2 kg) stewing beef, cubed
2 tablespoons (30 ml) seasoned flour
2 oz (50 g) butter
1 tablespoon (15 ml) soft dark brown sugar
1 tablespoon (15 ml) red wine vinegar
salt and pepper
16 oz (400 g) can of prunes, stoned and drained

Marinade
1 pint (500 ml) red wine
5 fl oz (125 ml) port
2 tablespoons (30 ml) olive oil
2 bay leaves
sprigs of thyme
1 tablespoon (15 ml) chopped fresh parsley
2 cloves garlic, crushed
10 oz (250 g) shallots, chopped

Mix the marinade ingredients, add the beef, and leave for 4 hours or overnight. Pre-heat the oven to 140°C/275°F/ Gas 1. Drain the beef, reserving the marinade, and put it in a plastic bag to coat with the flour. Fry in the butter until brown and then transfer to a casserole dish. Add the reserved marinade to the dish and bring to the boil. Add the sugar and vinegar and season. Cook in the pre-heated oven for 2½–3 hours. Stir in the prunes 30 minutes before the end of the cooking time. If a thicker sauce is desired, thicken with arrowroot or cornflour before serving.

Stir-fried celery and walnuts

My mother absolutely adores this as an accompaniment to beef casserole. Do try it – it's a perfect foil to the beef.

knob of butter
8 sticks celery, chopped diagonally
4 oz (100 g) walnut pieces
1 tablespoon (15 ml) soft dark brown sugar

Melt the butter and stir-fry the celery for 2 minutes. Add the walnuts and sugar and stir until the sugar caramelizes.

Sherried potatoes
Serves 6–8

2½ lb (1 kg) potatoes, diced and boiled
3 oz (75 g) butter
1 tablespoon (15 ml) soft dark brown sugar
pinch of nutmeg
1 egg, beaten
6 tablespoons (90 ml) medium dry sherry
salt and pepper

Pre-heat the oven to 190°C/375°F/Gas 5. Mash the cooked potatoes with the butter and sugar. Stir in the nutmeg, half the egg and the sherry. Season well. Spoon into an ovenproof serving dish, forking up the surface, brush with the remaining egg and cook in the pre-heated oven until the surface has browned.

Swede and orange purée
Serves 6–8

This is incredibly popular – it has a lovely texture and taste. It also keeps very well in a warm oven.

2–2½ lb (800 g–1 kg) swede, diced
1 oz (25 g) butter
3 tablespoons (45 ml) orange juice
4 tablespoons (60 ml) crème fraîche
salt and pepper

Boil, steam or microwave the swede until tender. Strain and mash with the butter. When smooth, add the orange juice and crème fraîche. Season well before serving. Can be kept, covered, in a warm oven for 30 minutes.

French beans and flaked hazelnuts
Serves 6–8

1½ lb (600 g) French beans
2 oz (50 g) flaked hazelnuts
2 teaspoons (10 ml) hazelnut oil

Top and tail the beans and boil, steam or microwave them until tender. Be careful not to overcook them, as they are better when they still have some 'bite'. Drain and add the hazelnuts and oil. Serve immediately.

Mincemeat parcels
Makes 12

This very simple alternative to mince pies is becoming increasingly popular.

1 packet filo pastry, defrosted
12 dessertspoons (120 ml) mincemeat (see page 209)
melted butter
icing or vanilla sugar to decorate

Pre-heat the oven to 190°C/375°F/Gas 5. Cut the filo pastry into 36 squares. Using a 12-hole bun tin, put 3 filo squares in each hole, layering them at a slight angle so that each parcel consists of a 12-pointed 'star'. Now put 1 dessertspoon of mincemeat into each parcel. Gather the pastry up so that each parcel encloses the mincemeat. Brush with melted butter. Cook in the pre-heated oven for 10–15 minutes until crisp and brown. Dust with the icing or vanilla sugar, and serve hot with ice-cream or cold with cream.

Christmas turkey
Serves 6–8

    14 lb (5.6 kg) oven-ready turkey
    stuffing (e.g. pork, chestnut and orange)
    butter
    salt and pepper
    streaky bacon (optional)

Stuff your turkey in the neck end. Pre-heat the oven to 220°C/425°F/Gas 7. Put a sheet of foil into a roasting tin and place the turkey on this. Smother with butter and season with salt and pepper. Cover the breasts with bacon if using (this helps keep them moist). Wrap the turkey loosely in the foil. Place in the pre-heated oven for 45 minutes, then reduce the temperature to 170°C/325°F/Gas 3 and cook for a further 3½ hours. Now unfold the foil, remove the bacon (this can be put back into the oven later and crisped up, ready to serve with the dinner). Turn the oven back up to 200°C/400°F/Gas 6 and cook for a further 30 minutes to brown the skin. Baste every 10 minutes during this period. Now leave in a warm place for 30–40 minutes before carving.

Pork, chestnut and orange stuffing

1lb (400 g) pork sausagemeat
12 oz (300 g) chestnuts, cooked and chopped
4 oz (100 g) fresh white breadcrumbs
1 onion, finely chopped
1 oz (25 g) butter
1 tablespoon (15 ml) chopped fresh parsley
grated rind and juice of 1 orange
1 egg, beaten
salt and pepper

Mix all the ingredients together and use to stuff your turkey.

Bread sauce
Serves 6–8

For many years I wouldn't even look at bread sauce, never mind try it. Then at a friend's house I finally succumbed and found what I had been missing out on. When it is properly made it is a lovely sauce, and I often serve it with roasted fowl.

½ an onion, studded with cloves
1 bay leaf
1 pint creamy milk
few black peppercorns
salt
2 oz (50 g) butter
3 oz (75 g) white breadcrumbs
2–3 tablespoons (30–45 ml) double cream

Put the onion with the bay leaf, milk, peppercorns and salt into a saucepan. Bring to the boil and then leave to stand for 20–30 minutes. Remove the bay leaf and add the breadcrumbs and half the butter. Cook on a low heat for 10 minutes until the breadcrumbs have swollen. You can now leave the sauce until needed. To finish, remove the onion. Re-heat gently, and add the remaining butter and cream just before serving.

Cranberry sauce
Serves 6–8

> 4 oz (100 g) sugar
> 5 fl oz (125 ml) water
> 10 oz (250 g) cranberries
> grated rind and juice of 1 orange
> 5 fl oz (125 ml) red wine
> 2 tablespoons (30 ml) port

Dissolve the sugar in the water. Add the cranberries, orange rind and juice, and red wine and simmer for 5–10 minutes until the cranberries have popped. Add the port just before serving. The sauce can be served hot or cold as preferred.

Brussels sprouts and chestnuts
Serves 6–8

No Christmas dinner would be complete without this dish.

> 1½ lb (600 g) Brussels sprouts
> 12 oz (300 g) chestnuts, cooked

Steam, microwave or boil the sprouts until tender. (If using fresh sprouts do not make a cross in the base, as this makes them go mushy.) When they are almost ready, mix in the chestnuts to warm through.

Christmas pudding
Makes a 2 pint (1.2 litre) pudding

I am very proud of this recipe and I can honestly (but not modestly!) say that I think it is the best pudding I have ever tasted.

    4 oz (100 g) vegetarian suet
    4 oz (100 g) fresh white breadcrumbs
    4 oz (100 g) mixed peel
    4 oz (100 g) glace cherries, chopped
    6 oz (150 g) soft dark brown sugar
    1¼ lb (500 g) mixed dried fruit
    1 teaspoon (5 ml) mixed spice
    pinch of nutmeg
    pinch of cinnamon
    grated rind of 1 lemon
    grated rind of 1 orange
    2 eggs, beaten
    6 tablespoons (90 ml) stout
    3 tablespoons (45 ml) dark rum
    3 tablespoons (45 ml) brandy
    silver tokens (optional)

Begin the pudding the day before you wish to steam it. Place all the ingredients except the tokens in a large mixing bowl and give them a good stir before leaving to marinade overnight. Next day, stir all the ingredients again – it is traditional for everyone to have a stir and to make a wish! If you are going to put silver tokens in your pudding, wrap them in greaseproof paper. Lightly grease your pudding basin with butter and pack the ingredients in, distributing the tokens throughout the pudding. Cover with a double layer of greaseproof paper and then with foil. Tie securely with string. Cook in the top of a steamer for 8 hours (remember to keep checking the simmering water level). Leave to cool completely and then replace with fresh greaseproof paper and foil. Store somewhere dark and cool until Christmas Day. To re-heat, steam for 2 hours.

Rum sauce
Serves 6–8

>2 oz (50 g) butter
>2 oz (50 g) plain flour
>15 fl oz (375 ml) creamy milk
>2 oz (50 g) caster sugar
>4 tablespoons (60 ml) dark rum
>5 fl oz (125 ml) double cream

Put the butter, flour and milk into a small saucepan and heat, stirring, until the sauce starts to thicken. Stir in the sugar and continue cooking for a few minutes. Add the rum and cream and stir well. Remove from the heat and cover the surface if keeping warm until required.

Brandy butter
Serves 6–8

>4 oz (100 g) softened butter
>2 oz (50 g) caster sugar
>2 oz (50 g) icing sugar
>4 tablespoons (60 ml) brandy

Cream all the ingredients together. Pile into a small dish and chill. Leave to harden before serving.

RUM BUTTER
Make as above, but substitute 2 oz (50 g) soft dark brown sugar for the caster sugar and rum for the brandy.

Trifle
Serves 6–8

I have always found my trifle to be a strong favourite with friends and family. I think it is something to do with the amount of alcohol that I add! You can make it with a custard powder, but this recipe does produce a very good custard. If you are a novice at home-made custard, just one word of warning. Cook your custard on a low heat and do not overcook it. Otherwise the egg starts to scramble!

8 trifle sponges
6 oz (150 g) raspberry jam
5 fl oz (125 ml) sherry, Madeira or marsala
20 ratafia biscuits, crumbled
12 oz–1 lb (300–400 g) fresh or canned fruit – banana and mango is good, or fresh raspberries

Custard
1 pint (500 ml) creamy milk
1 teaspoon (5 ml) vanilla essence
2 eggs plus 2 egg yolks, beaten
2 tablespoons (30 ml) caster sugar
1 teaspoon (5 ml) cornflour, mixed to a paste with a little milk

To decorate
10 fl oz (250 ml) whipping cream, whipped
whole ratafia biscuits
sugar violet and rose petals

Split the trifle sponges and sandwich back together with the jam. Place in a trifle bowl and sprinkle in the alcohol. Cover with crushed ratafia biscuits. To make the custard, bring the milk to the boil. Whisk together the other custard ingredients, pour on the milk, and return the mixture to the pan. Cook until it thickens, stirring well. Add the fruit to the trifle and pour the custard over. Chill. When cold, top with whipped cream and other decorations.

CUSTARD
The custard can be made separately and served hot with dishes such as apple pie.

Stuffed nut roast
Serves 6–8

Nutmeat
4 oz (100 g) pine-nuts
2 oz (50 g) cashews
2 oz (50 g) almonds
1 onion, chopped
1 oz (25 g) butter
4 tablespoons (60 ml) milk
2 eggs, beaten
4 oz (100 g) wholemeal breadcrumbs
pinch of nutmeg
salt and pepper

Stuffing
1 sachet vegetarian stuffing
4 oz (100 g) mushrooms, chopped
1 clove garlic, crushed
1 oz (25 g) butter
soy sauce
pinch of mixed herbs

Pre-heat the oven to 200°C/400°F/Gas 6. Grind the pine-nuts, cashews and almonds. Fry the onion in butter until soft. Mix together all the nutmeat ingredients. Make up the stuffing as directed on the packet. Cook the mushrooms and garlic in the butter until soft. Add to the stuffing and season with soy sauce and herbs. Grease a 1 lb (400 g) loaf tin. Put half the nutmeat into the tin and press down well. Cover with the stuffing and top with the rest of the nutmeat. Cover with foil and cook in the pre-heated oven for 1 hour. Remove the foil and cook for a further 10 minutes. Cool in the tin for 5 minutes before turning out. Can be served hot or cold.

Onion sauce
Serves 6–8

2 onions, chopped
2 tablespoons (30 ml) oil
2 tablespoons (30 ml) butter
1 tablespoon (15 ml) plain flour
2 teaspoons (10 ml) mushroom ketchup
few drops of gravy browning
1 pint (500 ml) boiling vegetable stock

Fry the onion in the oil and butter until browning. Stir in the flour and cook for 1 minute. Add the mushroom ketchup and gravy browning. Gradually blend in the stock and simmer for 5 minutes.

Mulled wine
Serves 6–10

This is often served in our house during the winter months. I have found that it keeps warm very well on the hot plate of a coffee filter – but do not actually put the wine through the coffee maker!

1 bottle red wine
10 fl oz (250 ml) dry cider
10 fl oz (250 ml) freshly squeezed orange juice
1 tablespoon (15 ml) port
1 tablespoon (15 ml) brandy
1 tablespoon (15 ml) soft dark brown sugar
2 cinnamon sticks
4 cloves
1 orange, sliced
1 lemon, sliced

Mix all the ingredients together and heat through gently, either on a hob or in the microwave. Serve in strong wine glasses or Irish coffee glasses.

Lamb in red wine
Serves 6–8

This is a very easy recipe which makes an excellent winter casserole. It's lovely served with creamed root vegetables to soak up the sauce.

>3 lb (1.2 kg) lean stewing lamb, cubed
>2 tablespoons (30 ml) olive oil
>2 onions, chopped
>4 cloves garlic, crushed
>12 fl oz (300 ml) red wine
>grated rind and juice of 2 oranges
>sprinkling of rosemary
>sprinkling of thyme
>salt and pepper

Marinade all the ingredients for 8 hours or overnight. Pre-heat the oven to 180°C/350°F/Gas 4. Tip everything into a casserole dish and bring to the boil. Cover and transfer to the pre-heated oven. Cook for 2 hours.

Christmas cake
Makes an 8 inch (20 cm) cake

1¼ lb (500 g) mixed dried fruit
10 oz (250 g) stoned raisins, chopped
2 oz (50 g) mixed peel
4 oz (100 g) glace cherries, chopped
2 tablespoons (30 ml) brandy
2 tablespoons (30 ml) Grand Marnier
8 oz (200 g) butter
8 oz (200 g) soft dark brown sugar
4 eggs, size 1
8 oz (200 g) plain flour
pinch of nutmeg
½ teaspoon (2.5 ml) mixed spice
2 oz (50 g) flaked toasted almonds, chopped
2 teaspoons (10 ml) black treacle
2 oz (50 g) plain cooking chocolate, melted
grated rind of ½ a lemon
grated rind of ½ an orange

Soak the mixed fruit, raisins, mixed peel and cherries in the alcohol overnight. Next day, pre-heat the oven to 140°C/275°F/Gas 1. Cream the butter and sugar together and then beat in the eggs, adding a little flour as you incorporate the eggs. Fold in the rest of the flour and the spices and then add all the fruit. Stir in other ingredients. Put into a greased and lined 8 inch (20 cm) round tin – tie a band of brown paper around the outside edge of the tin for extra protection. Cover the top of the cake with a layer of greaseproof paper. Bake in the pre-heated oven for 3½–4½ hours. It is done when a skewer inserted into the middle comes out clean. Leave to cool for 30 minutes in the tin before removing to a wire rack. When cold, 'feed' with more brandy and wrap in greaseproof paper before storing in an airtight container.

To marzipan this cake, you will need 1½ lb (600 g) of marzipan.

To ice the cake, you will need royal icing, made with 14 oz (350 g) icing sugar, 2 egg whites and 1 teaspoon (5 ml) glycerine.

Homemade mincemeat

Many, many years ago now I had an attempt at making both mincemeat and a Christmas pud. I don't remember where I got the recipes from – but neither were successful, both turning out quite dry, and now I realize that they didn't have a good proportion of fruit in them. So for many years I stuck to buying the shop-bought versions – I usually added a bit more alcohol to the mincemeat – and we were perfectly happy with them. Then about seven years ago, when I was made redundant in the run-up to Christmas, I decided I would have another go. This time, after looking at countless recipes, I decided to increase the amount of both fruit and alcohol just to see how they turned out. This time the results were magical! It is not essential to cook the mincement in this recipe – but it does help to distribute the fat from the suet evenly, ensuring that all the fruit is well covered. Even more important, the smell while it is cooking is absolutely heavenly!

10 oz (250 g) suet
1¼ lb (500 g) mixed dried fruit
10 oz (250 g) stoned raisins, chopped
8 oz (200 g) mixed peel
8 oz (200 g) glace cherries, chopped
12 oz (300 g) soft dark brown sugar
grated rind and juice of 1 orange
grated rind and juice of 1 lemon
grated rind and juice of 1 lime
1 tablespoon (15 ml) mixed spice
pinch of nutmeg
pinch of cinnamon
1 lb (400 g) Bramley apples, peeled, cored and
    chopped
4 tablespoons (60 ml) brandy
4 tablespoons (60 ml) Grand Marnier

Mix everything except the Grand Marnier in a large roasting dish, cover and leave overnight. Pre-heat the oven to its lowest setting, and bake for 2–3 hours. Stir occasionally to distribute the suet. Leave to cool, again stirring occasionally. When completely cool, stir in the Grand Marnier, pack into clean, dry jars, cover with wax discs and seal. I still sometimes add a little more brandy when using the mincemeat!

Index